The
HERB &
FLOWER
COOKBOOK

PLANT, GROW
AND EAT

PIP MCCORMAC

The
HERB &
FLOWER
COOKBOOK

PLANT, GROW
AND EAT

PIP MCCORMAC

Photography by Yuki Sugiura

Quadrille
PUBLISHING

Editorial director Jane O'Shea
Creative director Helen Lewis
Editor Louise McKeever
Designers Claire Peters, Emily Lapworth
Photographer Yuki Sugiura
Food stylist Alice Hart
Additional prop styling Emily Blunden
Production director Vincent Smith
Production controller Sarah Neesam

First published in 2014 by
Quadrille Publishing Limited
Alhambra House
27–31 Charing Cross Road
London WC2H 0LS
www.quadrille.co.uk

Text © 2014 Pip McCormac
Photography © 2014 Yuki Sugiura
Design and layout © 2014
Quadrille Publishing Limited

Cataloguing in Publication Data: a catalogue
record for this book is available from the
British Library.

ISBN 978 1 84949 416 8

Printed in China

For Nanna and Grandma, who both
loved flowers, though might have been
surprised I'd want to eat them.

Notes
All spoon measures are level unless
otherwise stated: 1 tsp = 5ml spoon;
1 tbsp = 15ml spoon.
Use medium eggs unless otherwise
suggested. Anyone who is pregnant or in
a vulnerable health group should avoid
recipes that use raw egg whites or lightly
cooked eggs.
If using the zest, buy unwaxed citrus fruit.
Timings are guidelines for conventional
ovens. If you are using a fan-assisted oven,
set your oven temperature approximately
15°C (1 Gas mark) lower.

Please note that not all the plants included
in the photographs in this book are edible.
Please make sure that you check when
buying your seeds and plants that they
are an edible variety. Violets (the viola
species) are edible; African violets
(*saintpaulia*) are not.

Introduction

It started with a pot of basil, bought ready grown from the supermarket. I was at university, going through an experimental phase that stretched well beyond kissing undesirables into tentatively trying out new flavour combinations. I plucked a few leaves, chopped them into a cheese sandwich and left the plant on my window ledge. The sandwich tasted amazing, the basil adding an exotically peppery hit. I began putting its leaves in everything – tomato sauces, steaming bowls of clams, roasts – the herb displayed proudly on my window ledge like a badge of civility, a green, leafy statement that I wasn't just your average student relying on beans on toast.

And that was when I made the discovery that looking after herbs is easy. I'd forget to water my plant, or Basil, as he inevitably became known, so he'd shrivel and droop. A splash of cold water later and he'd pick right up, his leaves would perk up again and he would start to fill the whole flat with his earthy aroma. I realised then that there was nothing to this, perhaps somewhat foolhardily. Look after plants and they flourish, neglect them and they die. That's all there is to it.

It's in that spirit that I've created this book – a belief that neither growing nor cooking should be hard work, but that both should be ultimately rewarding. There's an inner feeling of achievement that can only be gained from tending your own little garden, a glow that's made all the greater if you can use the fruits of your labour in your cooking.

None of the recipes in this book are very hard to make; they're all easy ideas given unusual flavour twists by using herbs and flowers that you might not otherwise have thought of. Any of these recipes can be made with any number of herbs – don't worry if you don't have the one I've suggested as I have always given at least three alternatives for you to use instead. Or don't use any herbs or flowers at all – they add depth of flavour and something different, but most of these recipes will work just as well without them. They are there to show off, to add a little variety, rather than because they're a necessity.

Similarly, don't worry if you don't have the time or inclination to grow them yourself. I'd argue with you if you claimed not to have the space, as almost anything will grow in a small pot on a window ledge, but of course you can buy any of these herbs from the shops, as I did with Basil, my first foray into container gardening. There's no shame in not growing your own. There is just a massive sense of satisfaction if you do.

Herb & Flower Thesaurus

There's a real joy in growing your own herbs and flowers, in using the fat of your land to add flavour to your cooking. Having spent an entire childhood avoiding anything to do with my parent's garden I've discovered the pride involved in snipping off a sprig and popping it straight into your pot.

And the best thing? It's really pretty easy. This guide is intended to show you how simple it is – if you're craving a more in-depth approach then there's plenty of information online, but this should be enough to get you started.

A few notes before you get out your trowel:

Soil – For herb and window boxes, the multi-use potting soil you buy in massive bags at DIY warehouses and garden centres will work just fine. Fill your boxes almost to the top, plant your seeds or cuttings and give them a really good drenching with water. Once a week, in summer months, it's worth giving them a capful or two of plant feed, available from the same places as the soil.

Containers – The larger your containers the better, though herbs can survive for shorter times in tiny pots of around 5cm diameter if you don't have much room. The ideal container gives each plant at least 10cm of space on all sides, to allow for roots and over ground growth. Put a layer of stones into the bottom before adding the soil, or make sure there are a couple of little holes in the bottom to allow for draining. Seeds and cuttings can be planted in containers outside unless otherwise stated.

Planting seeds – Unless the specific guidelines tell you otherwise, all you need to do is sprinkle a row of seeds over the top of the container, covering with a light dusting of soil and giving them a good water. As they start to shoot, separate any that are too close together, leaving a gap of at least 2.5cm between each plantlet. Then, after a couple of weeks, discard those that look a bit weedy and meek to leave room for the ones that are flourishing, this time with at least 5cm space between each.

Cuttings – Flowers like lavender and honeysuckle grow best from cuttings rather than seeds. Snip a healthy, non-flowering shoot from an existing plant – you want it to be around 5–10cm long. Keep only one or two pairs of leaves at the tip, dip the bottom in root power and poke the cutting into your container, leaving space around it. Water well and watch it grow. Once it's about 15cm high you should pinch off the top two leaves to encourage it to grow outwards – repeat this every ten days or so.

Plants – The fastest way to success, of course, is to buy plants from the garden centre and re-pot them. Squeeze them out of the pots they come in and gingerly break up the clump of earth that clings to their roots, taking care not to damage the roots. Place them into your container and pat some soil in around them. Water them well and you've got a ready-made garden that you can cook from straight away.

Basil

Tastes: Peppery and sweet.

When to plant: Late spring, starting off inside.

When to pick: Until late September, removing the leaves from growing stalks.

How to plant: Plant the seeds sparingly in small pots and cover with a very fine layer of soil; water well. Leave on a sunny windowsill. After about 5 weeks, move them outside, thinning the plants out until they are about 20cm apart. Basil needs sunshine and small amounts of water often, and will perk up quickly if it dries out a little. Pinch out the top leaves to stop it from growing too tall.

Plant it with: Mint, rosemary and thyme for a very fragrant box.

Works particularly well with: Chicken, pasta, Parmesan, salmon, peaches, tomatoes.

Substitute it with: Mint, lemon balm, oregano.

Can be eaten: Raw or steamed, although it can turn bitter if it is cooked for too long.

Borage

Tastes: Fresh and cucumber-like.

When to plant: From April to August.

When to pick: All the way up until November. You'll mainly want the edible blue flowers, but the leaves go in salads.

How to plant: Plant the seeds several centimetres apart, directly into the containers, in a spot that gets a little bit of shade. Cover with a thin layer of soil and water well. Borage doesn't like dry conditions, so make sure that the soil is kept moist, but not over-watered. Thin out to about 60cm apart and keep it as contained as possible – borage will take over your garden if you let it. The best thing, though, is that as a result it is almost impossible to kill.

Plant it with: Borage isn't very sociable. Keep it in a medium-sized container so it has space to grow without taking over from everything else.

Works particularly well with: Cantaloupe, dill, lemon, salmon, spring onions, strawberries, white fish.

Substitute it with: Parsley, basil, lemon thyme.

Can be eaten: Raw – it doesn't hold its flavour in cooking.

Calendula (Marigold)

Tastes: Peppery and radish-like.

When to plant: Early spring, any time after the last frost.

When to pick: Throughout the summer. Lopping off the flower heads will make the plant grow more replacements.

How to plant: Sow the seeds directly into the containers, covering them with a thin layer of soil – if you sew new seeds every three weeks or so you'll have a continual supply. Cover with a thin layer of soil; water well. It likes sunshine, water and any fertilising compost or plant feed you care to give it. Its roots are not deep, so one plant to a medium-sized container, or several in a larger one, about 20–40cm apart, will be fine. Just make sure it doesn't dry out.

Plant it with: Lavender, rosemary and mint all like similar conditions and will look really pretty together.

Works particularly well with: Beef, blue cheese, butter, celery, chilli, courgettes, olive oil, rice, salt.

Substitute it with: Nasturtium, thyme, sage.

Can be eaten: Raw, but works better cooked – oil and oily dishes bring out its full flavour.

Chervil

Tastes: Faintly like liquorice and similar to parsley.

When to plant: July or August.

When to pick: Late autumn to December. Cut off the leaves but leave at least 3cm of the stem to allow it to sprout again.

How to plant: Chervil will happily grow in small spaces, in tiny pots or slotted in amongst other herbs. Sew the seeds sparingly, about 5cm apart, and cover with a thin layer of compost, remembering to water well. Thin out to about 30cm apart. Chervil prefers shade and doesn't like too much heat, so planting it under existing taller plants is a good idea – just make sure that the soil is always a little bit wet.

Plant it with: Sage, basil, oregano or anything with thick leaves that will help to protect it from the sun.

Works particularly well with: Asparagus, duck, fennel, green beans, lamb, potatoes, salmon, trout.

Substitute it with: Parsley, oregano, basil.

Can be eaten: Raw or cooked in sauces.

Clockwise from opposite top left: Various; hibiscus; coriander; rosemary, African violet, lemon thyme; various; geranium

Chive

Tastes: Strongly like onion.

When to plant:
Early spring to midsummer.

When to pick: After a couple of months it will have grown enough for you to be able to slice off most of the chive, leaving just 2cm to grow back. Chopping off the edible flower head will encourage more to grow.

How to plant: Start growing the chives inside, sprinkling the seeds in a row and then barely covering with soil. Water them well and move them outside once they're 5–6cm tall – you can carefully dig them up and transplant them to another container if you like, spacing them about 15cm apart. Although it might disappear in the winter it is still alive – you can leave it outside and it'll grow back again in the spring.

Plant it with: It tends to grow pretty tall, so plant it with squat, equally reedy herbs like dill and thyme.

Works particularly well with:
Beetroot, chicken, haddock, goat's cheese, parsnip, potatoes, sour cream.

Substitute it with:
Basil, oregano, winter savory.

Can be eaten:
Raw, steamed or cooked in sauces.

Coriander

Tastes: Fresh and citrus-like.

When to plant:
Late spring to the end of August.

When to pick: From June through the winter you can tear the leaves off in as big a clump as you would like.

How to plant: Make a shallow line-shaped groove in the soil and sprinkle the seeds into it, aiming for a bit of space between each one. Cover with a thin layer of soil and water well. Thin out to 20cm apart once the seedlings are established. Coriander likes sun but gets burnt and brown in too much heat, so a spot with a bit of shade is ideal. It doesn't grow back particularly strongly after picking the leaves, so plant a new row of seeds every month or so to give you a continual supply.

Plant it with: It needs a good amount of water, so pair it with mint, oregano or chives.

Works particularly well with:
Carrots, chicken, green salad, peanuts, prawns, watermelon, white cabbage.

Substitute it with:
Mint, basil, lemon balm.

Can be eaten: Raw or cooked in sauces. The seeds can be sprinkled over salads too, or ground to make rubs for meat.

Dill

Tastes: Soft and sweet, and similar to caraway.

When to plant:
From April until the end of July.

When to pick: Snip off the whole stalk from mid June until late September.

How to plant: Fill a small or medium-sized container with soil and create a groove down the middle with the end of a pencil or your finger. Sprinkle the seeds into the groove and cover with about 1cm of soil. Water it well and watch the sprouts begin to grow – you can carefully uproot them if you need to give them more space, they like at least 10cm in each direction if possible. Sow a fresh batch every month or so for a continual harvest throughout the summer.

Plant it with: Dill needs a lot of space, so keep it by itself or with a similarly thin herb that won't branch into it, such as chives.

Works particularly well with:
Cucumber, lime, lemon, gherkins, mackerel, red peppers, spring onions, trout.

Substitute it with:
Borage, chervil, parsley.

Can be eaten: Raw or cooked in sauces.

Geranium
(Pelargonium)

Tastes: Subtly floral.

When to plant:
April, starting them off indoors.

When to pick: Break off the scented leaves from summer until late autumn.

How to plant: Fill a pot with soil and sprinkle over a few seeds of a scented-leaved geranium, leaving about 2.5cm between them. Cover with a dusting of soil, try to keep it all quite loose. Add a bit of water and some liquid fertiliser and set on a sunny windowsill for a few weeks. Once sprouted, and spring's temperamental weather is out the way, move them outside – they like a lot of sunshine, so put them in the brightest spot. Don't water too often; check the soil with your finger and if it's still moist, leave them be. Chop off any dead heads or brown leaves, and bring them back indoors at the end of September, to the sunniest part of your house.

Plant it with: It is best kept on its own, but it looks pretty when you include different varieties and colours.

Works particularly well with:
Lemon, melon, raspberries, sponge cake, strawberries.

Substitute it with: Rose, violet, savory.

Can be eaten: Cooked – its leaves give off its flavour at high temperatures.

Clockwise from top left: Chervil; mustard flowers; various; thyme, sage, mint; savory; thyme, lavender, rosemary

Hibiscus

Tastes: Fresh and ever so slightly floral.

When to plant: Spring.

When to pick: Pick off the edible flower heads throughout summer and autumn, this will encourage more to bloom.

How to plant: It's best to buy a baby hibiscus plant rather than try to grow it from seed. Plant the shrub in a container at least 20cm in diameter and 20cm deep, patting soil in around the root ball and leaving the top 2cm of it exposed. Hibiscus likes a lot of sun, so grow it in a container you can easily move around into the light. Don't over-water; check the soil with your finger for dryness before you add more. Prune any yellow or brown leaves, and move it back indoors for winter – it's very hardy and should survive happily by a sunny window.

Plant it with: Because its roots grow so wide, it should be kept in its own container.

Works particularly well with: Chilli, carrots, cinnamon, ginger, pork, mangoes, milk, oranges, tomatoes.

Substitute it with: Mint, violet, honeysuckle.

Can be eaten: Raw, dried or boiled in teas and sauces.

Honeysuckle

Tastes: Sweet, like honey.

When to plant: Spring.

When to pick: Pick off the edible flower heads from high summer all the way through to mid-autumn.

How to plant: Growing from seed is tricky, so it's much easier to start from cuttings. These will grow up trellises and walls very happily in sunlight. If your variety is a climber, plant the cutting in a deep container next to a wall in full sunlight. If it's a bush variety, plant it anywhere that gets a lot of warmth. Add a touch of root grow stimulator to the base of the cutting and keep its soil well watered. Prune the flowers to keep it the shape and size you want, as honeysuckle tends to ramble and take over...which is really part of its charm.

Plant it with: Honeysuckle needs space to grow but it will attract bees, so plant lavender nearby to really draw them to your edible garden.

Works particularly well with: Blackberries, blackcurrants, honey, ginger, maple syrup, mint.

Substitute it with: Mint, hibiscus, rose.

Can be eaten: Raw or boiled in sauces and teas.

Jasmine

Tastes: Delicate and tea-like.

When to plant: Spring, after the last frost.

When to pick: Chop off the edible flowers throughout the summer.

How to plant: Buy a jasmine vine from a garden centre and replant in a larger pot for a few weeks. Then choose a deep container, at least 40cm tall, with a hole in the bottom for drainage. Put some pebbles into the bottom of the container and soak the root ball well with water before dropping it into the pot so that the root is 3cm from the top. Surround it with soil. Jasmine loves sunshine, so plant it in a bright spot that is sheltered from the wind, preferably in front of a wall or trellis for it to creep up. Keep it well watered and moist.

Plant it with: Keep jasmine alone in its container. However, the creeping plant will provide good shade for herbs such as borage or chervil nearby.

Works particularly well with: Chard, goat's cheese, lemon, salmon, tomatoes.

Substitute it with:
Lilac, nasturtium, thyme.

Can be eaten: Raw or boiled in teas.

Lavender

Tastes: As it smells – floral and sweet.

When to plant: Late winter, starting it off indoors first.

When to pick: The edible flower heads can be picked from late spring throughout the summer. More will grow in their place.

How to plant: Cuttings are the easiest way to grow lavender – you want a 10cm side stalk that isn't flowering. Strip off the bottom leaves and dip the cut end into a root growth stimulator. Plant it at a 5cm depth in a small pot of gritty compost and keep it inside on a sunny windowsill. Keep it well watered. Replant in a bigger pot and move it outside after a month or so, once it has really started to grow. Leave it somewhere sunny and water it every day throughout the summer, lopping off any dead heads or leaves. It is fairly hardy and will grow as long as you let it – remove the older stems as they get woody and let the new stems keep replenishing themselves.

Plant it with: Sun-loving, thirsty plants such as rosemary, mint and savory.

Works particularly well with: Apricots, beef, lemon, pork, peaches, raspberries.

Substitute it with:
Violet, rosemary, savory.

Can be eaten: Raw, roasted or boiled in sauces and teas.

Clockwise from opposite top left: Sorrel; geranium; rose, lavender; basil

Lemon Balm

Tastes: Cool and lemony.

When to plant: Early to late spring, starting it off indoors first.

When to pick: Handfuls of leaves can be picked off until the very end of autumn.

How to plant: Sew the seeds in small pots, cover with just a tiny amount of soil, water well and leave on a sunny windowsill for a few weeks. Once they have sprouted and the weather has got a bit warmer, choose the strongest plants, uproot them carefully and replant in pots outside with 10–15cm between each one. Place in a sunny and sheltered spot. Water well throughout the summer and pick the leaves as often as you need – they grow back quickly. Leave out all winter as it should happily spring back into life the following year.

Plant it with: Its fresh fragrance will offset more pungent herbs such as chives, but it will get on well with anything that likes sunshine.

Works particularly well with: Chicken, courgettes, cucumber, Parmesan, peas, trout.

Substitute it with: Lemon thyme, basil, parsley.

Can be eaten: Raw or very lightly cooked and added to pans just before serving.

Lemon Thyme

Tastes: Woody and lemony.

When to plant: Spring.

When to pick: Early summer until late autumn.

How to plant: Lemon thyme will spread quite wide, so plant the seeds about 10cm apart in a shallow well of soil, covering with just a little sprinkling of extra soil, water well. It likes a lot of sun, water and shelter, and is pretty hardy if it is placed somewhere it can get all three of these. It will flower in high summer, and the flowers can be eaten too, just chop them off and sprinkle them into salads or over meats. The more you pick lemon thyme sprigs the more you will encourage it to grow, so don't be afraid of hacking away at the leaves or of discarding any woody stalks.

Plant it with: Its fragrance and sun-worshipping nature make it an ideal partner for lavender, rosemary and regular thyme.

Works particularly well with: Apples, chicken, courgettes, elderflower, ginger, pears, turkey.

Substitute it with: Lemon balm, thyme, rosemary.

Can be eaten: Raw, roasted, cooked in sauces or steamed with vegetables.

Lilac

Tastes: More peppery than floral, not unlike radish.

When to plant: Spring to early summer.

When to pick: The edible flower heads can be picked all through the summer.

How to plant: You'll want to start this off from a baby plant bought in a garden centre. You will need a larger pot with a hole in the bottom for drainage. Put some pebbles into the bottom of the container and soak the root ball well with water before planting. Choose a sunny spot and don't overcrowd – it likes a lot of space in its pot. If you never let the soil get soggy and you remove any dead heads, then the lilac should bloom very happily, just give it a drop of plant food every couple of weeks in the spring and summer to keep it strong.

Plant it with: It prefers its own pot and space, but it is so colourful that you can plant it near lavender and nasturtiums to make a really pretty collection.

Works particularly well with: Blackberries, blackcurrants, cream cheese, grouse, lemon, sea bass.

Substitute it with: Nasturtium, calendula, thyme.

Can be eaten: Raw, cooked or stewed.

Lovage

Tastes: Salty and fresh, like celery.

When to plant: March through to early summer.

When to pick: From May until mid-winter.

How to plant: Create a 2cm deep groove in the soil with your finger. Sew the lovage seeds about 3cm apart, cover with a thin layer of soil and water lightly. Thin them out as they grow, so there is about 10cm between each plant, and water fairly sparingly, keeping the soil damp but not soaked. Lovage can grow really tall unless you prune it regularly – snip the leaves off when you need them and cut it right back in June to encourage further growth. The leaves taste best when they're young, so don't be afraid to hack at larger plants.

Plant it with: Parsley, basil and oregano.

Works particularly well with: Celery, cherries, duck, lettuce, lemon, pasta, red peppers.

Substitute it with: Parsley, borage, oregano.

Can be eaten: Raw or cooked in soups and sauces.

Clockwise from opposite top left: Lavender, rosemary; various; honeysuckle; various; sage; mint, basil, coriander; thyme, rosemary

Marjoram

Tastes: Sweet and pungent, similar to oregano but slightly stronger.

When to plant: Spring.

When to pick: Chop off the leaves before the plant flowers in late summer.

How to plant: Create a 2cm deep groove in the soil with your finger. Plant the seeds in a row about 5cm apart. Cover with a very thin layer of earth and water well. You'll need to keep the soil moist for the first couple of weeks until the seed sprouts, then you can start to water less. Marjoram likes sunny climates, so keep it somewhere warm and sheltered, and just prune off the leaves when you need it. It doesn't usually survive British winters, so either let it die off or bring its container indoors and leave it on a sunny ledge until the following spring.

Plant it with: Basil and oregano have the same desire for sunshine and don't like too much water.

Works particularly well with: Butternut squash, fennel, lamb, onion, pasta, potatoes, spinach.

Substitute it with: Oregano, basil, sage.

Can be eaten: Raw or cooked gently in sauces.

Mint

Tastes: Cool and minty.

When to plant: Spring to late summer.

When to pick: Late spring to late autumn, and through the winter if it is brought indoors.

How to plant: Mint has large roots that can fill a big container, so it's best to plant it by itself. Plant the seeds 5cm deep and at least 5cm apart in a very large container. Discard those that are the least promising once they start sprouting. You need to water it occasionally as it begins to grow, but after that you can leave it to its own devices, only giving it more water during extended droughts. Pick leaves from the top of the plant for eating and once the mint is about 25–30cm tall, start pinching out the top leaves to stop the mint growing up any further. Bring it indoors in the winter and it should keep going as long you let it.

Plant it with: Best on its own or with deep rooted herbs like basil and rosemary.

Works particularly well with: Broad bean, cucumber, lamb, lime, mangoes, peas, peaches, prawns.

Substitute it with: Lemon balm, parsley, lovage.

Can be eaten: Raw, cooked in sauces or stewed in tea.

Mustard

Tastes: Hot and peppery.

When to plant: Spring.

When to pick: All year round –
it should survive most frosts.

How to plant: Create a 0.5cm deep
groove in the soil with your finger. Drop
the seeds into the soil, about 2.5cm apart,
and dust with only the lightest covering
of earth. Water it regularly – it likes cool
weather and needs to be kept moist, so a
shady spot is ideal. Thin out to about 15cm
apart once the seeds have sprouted. Chop
off the flowers of younger plants for use
in salads or stews, and snip the leaves off
older plants for salads in place of rocket.
During really cold spells it may need to be
brought indoors, but some varieties, such
as black mustard, thrive on a snap
of freezing weather.

Plant it with: Tall herbs that will offer it
shade, such as coriander and oregano.

Works particularly well with:
Bacon, beef, chicken, garlic,
goose, ham, potatoes, radish.

Substitute it with:
Nasturtium, winter savory, thyme.

Can be eaten: Raw or stewed in sauces.

Nasturtium

Tastes: Peppery, with a hint of citrus.

When to plant: Early spring,
starting it off indoors first.

When to pick: All summer long, until late
September. The seeds in the dead heads
can be used like capers.

How to plant: Start them off indoors on
a sunny windowsill. Fill a medium-sized
container with soil and plant the seeds
about 3cm deep, 8–10 seeds to a pot.
Cover with a thin layer of soil and water
well. Water them regularly and after about
a month choose the two or three sprouts
that look the strongest and discard the rest.
Move the pot outside to as sunny a spot as
possible and don't add any fertiliser, as they
bloom better without it. Cut off any dead
heads throughout the summer and the
plants probably won't need any pruning.

Plant it with: Nasturtium tends to ramble,
so keep it alone or go for fairly contained
herbs such as chives.

Works particularly well with:
Artichoke, cabbage, celery, white fish.

Substitute it with:
Calendula, thyme, basil.

Can be eaten:
Raw or steamed with vegetables.

Clockwise from top left: Chervil; various; chive; thyme; savory, parsley; sage, African violets, rosemary

Oregano

Tastes: Like a milder version of basil.

When to plant: Spring.

When to pick: Cut off the leaves all summer long, this will encourage more growth.

How to plant: Create a 3cm deep groove in the soil with your finger. Plant the seeds in the groove, cover with soil and a light sprinkling of water, and place the pot in an area that gets a lot of sunlight. As the shoots begin to sprout, thin them out so that they are about 10cm apart, discarding the weediest stalks. Water it frequently and pinch out the top leaves once they reach about 20–25cm. Chop off any flower buds before they bloom as they will weaken the flavour of the leaves. Prune oregano right back to just a couple of tiers of leaves and cover with mulch in the winter – it can last anywhere from two to four years.

Plant it with: Chervil, coriander and lavender.

Works particularly well with: Ham, lamb, mozzarella, mushrooms, sausage, sea bass, tomatoes.

Substitute it with: Basil, marjoram, chervil.

Can be eaten: Raw or cooked in sauces.

Pansy

Tastes: Vaguely salty and slightly peppery, with an underlying savoury flavour.

When to plant: Late spring to mid summer.

When to pick: Remove the edible flower heads throughout the summer.

How to plant: If it's still quite cool outside start the pansies off indoors, otherwise plant them straight into a container in a really sunny spot. Make a series of 2cm deep holes in the soil using your finger, put a seed into each and cover with soil. Keep the soil well watered and the seeds should sprout within about three weeks. The more times you pick off the flowers for salads the more they'll grow, so don't be afraid to really attack them. Lop off any brown leaves and if you keep them well watered they should do well all season.

Plant it with: Other sun-loving plants such as rosemary, lavender and thyme.

Works particularly well with: Cabbage, carrot, coriander, lime, radishes, trout, tuna.

Substitute it with: Nasturtium, calendula, thyme.

Can be eaten: Raw in salads.

Parsley

Tastes: Like peppery grass.

When to plant: Spring.

When to pick: All summer and into autumn, chopping off the stalks and leaves whenever you need them.

How to plant: Because parsley seeds are tough, the trick is to soak them in boiling water for a day before you plant them to break down their exterior. Drain the water away and sprinkle the seeds lightly over the top of your soil, mixing them gently into the surface with your finger. Place the pot in a relatively sunny spot. Water them well, keeping them moist as they sprout and thinning them out if you have too many. It needs a gap of at least 5cm either side of each to flourish properly. Parsley usually lasts for two years if you bring the container indoors over the winter – you should get pretty flowers in its second season.

Plant it with: Oregano, basil, lemon balm.

Works particularly well with:
Cod, lemon, ham, haddock, mint, Parmesan, potatoes.

Substitute it with:
Lemon balm, oregano, basil.

Can be eaten: Raw or cooked in sauces.

Purslane

Tastes: Slightly sour and slightly salty.

When to plant: April through to August.

When to pick: Snip off the leaves throughout the summer until early autumn.

How to plant: Create a series of 1cm deep holes in the soil with your finger. Sow the seeds into the holes, cover with a thin layer of soil and water well. Place the container in a sunny spot. Keep watering regularly and you should be able to pick the leaves in less than two months. Purslane will survive in fairly dry conditions, so it is ideal if you want a low-maintenance herb. Just thin out the shoots so that there is about 10cm between each one, using the weedier plants as micro-greens in a salad. Plant a new crop every month to keep you going throughout the summer.

Plant it with: Lavender, rosemary, sorrel.

Works particularly well with:
Apple, mangetout, mango, peas, pear, salmon.

Substitute it with:
Borage, lemon balm, mint.

Can be eaten:
Raw or cooked lightly in sauces.

Clockwise from top left: Parsley; mint; geranium; sage; rosemary, chives, lavender; sage, African violets, rosemary

Rosemary

Tastes: Pungently aromatic, and similar to pine needles.

When to plant: Late spring.

When to pick: Year round, cutting off 8–10cm sprigs.

How to plant: Although you can grow rosemary from seed, its success rate is so low that it's best to pot from an existing plant. Dig a hole in a container that is slightly larger and deeper than the pot it came in. Add about 1cm of sand to the hole and put the plant on top, filling it in with the soil you dug out. It won't need much care – just water if it completely dries out and trim the side stems to keep it the size you want. The rosemary will grow as large as you'll let it and should last for up to 20 years with only minimal pruning.

Plant it with: Other deep-rooted perennial herbs such as thyme, basil and mint.

Works particularly well with: Apple, beef, butternut squash, cherries, grapefruit, lamb, lemon, oranges.

Substitute it with: Sage, thyme, savory.

Can be eaten: Raw or cooked and roasts well.

Sage

Tastes: Earthy and strong.

When to plant: Early spring or throughout the summer.

When to pick: From late spring until late autumn.

How to plant: Create 1cm deep grooves in the soil with your finger. Sprinkle the seeds into the grooves, cover with soil and water well. They should start to shoot up after 2 weeks and have leaves ready to pick after about a month. Thin to 40–55cm apart. When they are young they need a lot of water, but once they get bigger you can leave them in the sunshine and they'll thrive – just make sure you water them when they get dry. Sage tends to grow outwards and take over containers, so chop off leaves regularly to keep it the size you want – it's very hardy and will grow back no matter how ruthlessly you prune it.

Plant it with: Rosemary, basil and oregano.

Works particularly well with: Apple, capers, egg, green beans, lamb, pork, tomatoes.

Substitute it with: Marjoram, basil, nasturtium.

Can be eaten: Raw, but it's better when lightly cooked in sauces.

Sorrel

Tastes: Lemony.

When to plant: March to May.

When to pick: Snip off the young leaves from spring through to November.

How to plant: Create 0.5cm deep ridges in the soil using your finger. Sow the seeds, cover them with a sprinkling of soil and water well. Leave the container in a sunny but sheltered spot. Once the seeds have started sprouting, thin them out so there is 7–8cm between each. A few weeks later, once they start to get really thick, thin them out again so that there is a 30cm gap between each one. Regularly prune back the older, larger leaves – they're less tasty anyway and this will encourage new growth. Keep the ground fairly well watered in sunny periods, and you should have a very healthy, happy herb on your hands.

Plant it with: Lavender, rosemary and purslane.

Works particularly well with: Chicken, courgettes, cucumber, orange, strawberries, sea bass, sole.

Substitute it with: Lemon thyme, lemon balm, mint.

Can be eaten: Raw, cooked or roasted.

Summer Savory

Tastes: Woody and aromatic, similar to rosemary.

When to plant: March until August.

When to pick: You can pick the leaves as soon as they sprout, until about October.

How to plant: Create 1cm deep grooves in the soil and scatter the seeds into them, covering with a light dusting of earth. Position the container in a sunny spot and water fairly well, continuing to do so to prevent it from drying out. It can grow outwards and take over, so thin the shoots out so that there is a 12cm space between each one. Regularly prune the leaves, pinching them back to encourage new growth. It's pretty hard to kill, so as long as it gets light and water it should be fine.

Plant it with: Lavender, sorrel and oregano.

Works particularly well with: Beef, grapefruit, onions, orange, pork, rice, sweet potato.

Substitute it with: Rosemary, winter savory, thyme.

Can be eaten: Raw, roasted, dried or cooked in sauces.

Clockwise from top left: Rosemary, pansy; various; various; chervil; chervil; rosemary, sage

PIP'S BALCONY

COCKTAIL HERB BAR

Tarragon

Tastes: Fragrant, like anise.

When to plant: Spring to late summer.

When to pick: Late spring until late autumn. Snip off the stalks and pinch the leaves.

How to plant: Tarragon is one of the easiest herbs to look after – it is hardy and doesn't need much care. It likes a bit of shade, so choose a spot that gets some light but also some respite from the sun. Plant the seeds in shallow dips in the soil, cover with a light dusting of earth and water frequently, making sure it doesn't dry out. Thin the plants out so that there is 10cm between each one. Either let it die off in the winter, or bring it indoors where it will live happily on a sunny windowsill.

Plant it with: Chervil, coriander and chive.

Works particularly well with: Chicken, lemon, green peppers, mushrooms, potatoes.

Substitute it with: Oregano, lemon balm, chervil.

Can be eaten: Raw, roasted or in sauces.

Thyme

Tastes: Pungently woody.

When to plant: April and throughout the summer.

When to pick: Harvest the leaves from mid summer through to late autumn.

How to plant: Thyme likes a lot of sun, so it's best to wait until the spring is well underway and the ground has warmed up after the winter. Create 1cm deep grooves in the soil with your finger. Plant the seeds in the grooves and cover them with a light sprinkling of soil. Thyme doesn't need too much water, so just make sure it doesn't completely dry out and it should thrive. Pinch back the leaves to stop it from taking over the container – a fully-grown plant needs at least a 10cm gap between each one. You can leave them out in the winter, just prune them back to encourage growth.

Plant it with: Lemon thyme, lavender and rosemary.

Works particularly well with: Apple, artichoke, cheddar cheese, lamb, lemon, ginger, rhubarb, sausage, strawberries.

Substitute it with: Savory, rosemary, nasturtium.

Can be eaten: Raw, cooked or roasted.

Violet
(Viola species)

Tastes: Floral and slightly soapy.

When to plant: Autumn.

When to pick: Late winter through to early summer.

How to plant: You can buy violet plants from the garden centre, but if you are starting from seed then plant them when the weather starts to cool. Do not buy African violets (*saintpaulia*) as they are inedible. Make 2cm deep holes in the soil that are at least 5–10cm apart. Sew the seeds and cover with a thin layer of soil. Water immediately, but then leave them over the winter to quietly germinate. Once they flower in the spring (or late winter if you're lucky), keep them well watered and pick off the flowers and leaves for use in salads or desserts, which will encourage more growth.

Plant it with: As the herbs begin to die off in the autumn, replace them with violets – you can switch them back the following summer.

Works particularly well with: Cream, cinnamon, grapefruit, lemon, plums.

Substitute it with: Rose, lavender, geranium.

Can be eaten: Raw or cooked.

Winter Savory

Tastes: Peppery. It is a stronger version of summer savory.

When to plant: September.

When to pick: All through the winter.

How to plant: As its name suggests, winter savory can survive very cold climates, and will even be ok under a snowfall. Create 1cm deep grooves in the soil using your finger. Shake the seeds into the grooves, covering with a light sprinkling of soil. Water it straight away and then let the autumnal weather keep the soil moist – only top it up with water if there is an unseasonable dry spell. Thin out the plants so that there are at least 10cm gaps between each one and hack at the leaves as much as you like, it will keep growing back as long as you let it. It is perennial, meaning it should keep going, as long as you give it some shade in the summer.

Plant it with: Violet, parsley and sage.

Works particularly well with: Apple, carrot, garlic, pear, sausage, white bean.

Substitute it with: Summer savory, rosemary, thyme.

Can be eaten: Raw, roasted or cooked in sauces.

Breakfast

Admittedly real breakfasts – the kind with pots of coffee, vats of juice, piles of papers and nostalgic music on the radio – only really happen at the weekend. But that doesn't mean that the rest of the week's mornings can't include a few snatched seconds to blitz together a smoothie, spoon a few ready-poached apricots into a bowl or smother some bread in orange curd before legging it out of the door.

Herbs and flowers are at their most fragrant in the morning, the cool night air softening them slightly and encouraging them to release their aromas as the sun begins to shine. There should be nothing more natural than plucking a few leaves out of your box, sprinkling them into your morning dish and then going about your day, energised and slightly smug that you've not simply had a latte for sustenance. These fuss-free recipes are all about little hints of flavour that will set you up for the day.

Rosemary Poached
RED GRAPEFRUIT

SERVES: **2**
COOKING TIME: **30-35 MINUTES**

1 red grapefruit | 1 sprig of rosemary | 3 tbsp Demerara sugar
3 tbsp smooth orange juice | 1 tbsp balsamic vinegar
2 tbsp olive oil | Crème fraîche, for serving

Grapefruit segments are a classic breakfast, but I've always found them to be a little too tart in the morning. The sweet juices here will make the fruit much more palatable – you can eat the skins as they go soft on roasting, but that's entirely up to you. Make them in bulk and keep them in the fridge for a day or two if you like, as they're just as nice completely cold.

Thoroughly wash the grapefruit and cut it into quarters, leaving the skin on. Place the wedges into a small roasting dish. Preheat the oven to 180°C/Gas mark 4.

Pull the leaves off the rosemary sprig and throw them into the bottom of a mixing jug or bowl, with the sugar, orange juice, vinegar and olive oil. Beat them together lightly with a fork and pour the mixture over the grapefruit.

Roast the fruit in the oven for 25 minutes. Remove the grapefruit with a slotted spoon and place on a plate to cool. Pour the cooking juices into a small saucepan and bring to the boil for 5–10 minutes or until thick and syrupy.

Divide the grapefruit segments between two bowls and pour over the syrup. Add a dollop of crème fraîche to each and serve immediately.

Substitute the
rosemary with...
THYME, LAVENDER,
SUMMER SAVORY

Orange and Summer Savory
CURD

MAKES: **ABOUT 400ML**
COOKING TIME: **15 MINUTES**

4 egg yolks | Zest and juice of 2 small oranges
Juice of 2 limes | 225g caster sugar | 115g butter
2 sprigs of summer savory, leaves only

This recipe was originally created by the great food writer Sybil Kapoor. Her simple idea to take the classic lemon curd and reinvent it with oranges was pure genius. I've adapted it by adding herbs and some lime juice, both of which give it a more piquant tang. It makes for a very indulgent breakfast smothered over crusty white bread, spooned into Greek yoghurt or over porridge. On bread, I like to use a butter that is slightly salted for a rich contrast to the sweetness of the jam.

Preheat the oven to 140°C/Gas mark 1. Wash an empty jam jar in hot soapy water, rinse it out and place it in the oven to sterilise whilst it dries.

Meanwhile, put all the ingredients into a saucepan and cook over a medium heat, stirring regularly, for 15 minutes. Pour the mixture into the jar – it will look quite runny but don't worry, it will set as it cools – and cover it with a waxed disk of paper (I never have any professional ones to hand, so I just cut a circle from baking paper).

Once the jam has cooled, screw the top on firmly. It will keep in the fridge for a couple of weeks once opened.

Substitute the
summer savory
with...
ROSEMARY, THYME,
LEMON THYME

Apple, Elderflower and Thyme
MUFFINS

---•---

MAKES: **12**
COOKING TIME: **25 MINUTES**

---•---

300g self-raising flour | 300g caster sugar | A pinch of salt
100ml elderflower cordial | 100ml milk | 1 egg | 100g butter, melted
4 Cox apples, peeled, cored and finely diced | 2 sprigs of thyme, leaves only
Demerara sugar, for sprinkling

Muffins are the most American of breakfast fare, but these work well as a mid-morning snack, paired with a large cup of coffee. They're indulgent, weekend food, something to eat at a sunny table rather than whilst hurriedly rushing out the door to work. The elderflower cordial ensures that they are moist all the way through and the thyme stops them from being sickly sweet.

Preheat the oven to 180°C/Gas mark 4. In a mixer, beat together all the ingredients apart from the demerara sugar until a smooth paste has formed – it will be a bit gooier than conventional cake mixtures.

Line a muffin tray with 12 individual muffin cases and spoon some of the mixture into each one, filling them almost to the top. Sprinkle a few grains of demerara sugar on top of each and bake in the oven for 25 minutes, until brown on top and springy to the touch. Leave to cool slightly in the tin before lifting out and leaving to cool on a wire cooling rack. They're best when warm and fresh, but they will keep for 2–3 days in an airtight container.

Substitute the thyme with...
LEMON THYME, ROSEMARY, OREGANO

Best Ever Minty
BREAKFAST SMOOTHIE

SERVES: **2**
PREPARATION TIME: **5 MINUTES**

1 overripe mango | 100g ripe strawberries, hulled | 2 sprigs of mint, leaves only
2 cardamom pods | 200g low-fat natural yoghurt
1 tbsp agave syrup or runny honey

It's a bold claim, but the delicately fragrant flavour of the cardamom next to the cool and energising zing of mint really is the perfect morning combo. You can play around with whatever fruit you want to add, but I like the sweetness of overripe mangoes and strawberries, which feel like they wake you up soothingly.

Peel and chop the mango, removing and discarding the stone and skin. Put the mango flesh into a food processor with the strawberries and mint leaves and blitz to a purée.

Carefully insert the tip of a sharp knife into one end of the cardamom pods and use the knife to split them open. Discard the pods and add the cardamom seeds, yoghurt and agave or honey to the food processor. Blitz again until combined.

You will end up with about 500ml of smoothie. Divide between 2 glasses and drink immediately.

Substitute the mint with...
LEMON THYME,
LEMON BALM, SORREL

*Substitute the
lavender with...*
ROSEMARY, MINT,
VIOLET PETALS

Lavender
POACHED APRICOTS

---·---

SERVES: **2**
COOKING TIME: **15 MINUTES**

---·---

150g apricots **|** 1 tbsp caster sugar
1 sprig of lavender **|** Greek yoghurt, for serving

This breakfast is lovely, as it is sweet and light. You can make larger quantities at a time if you like, just keep them in a container in the fridge for up to a week. Be sparing with the lavender, as you want it to add to the flavour of the fruit rather than overpower it. You could also add some fresh berries; I find that a few raspberries work well.

Halve and stone the apricots. Place the apricot halves into a small saucepan with a lid and add 50ml cold water, the sugar and the flowers from the sprig of lavender (if you're using dried lavender, ½ tsp will do).

Bring the apricots to the boil, then cover them with a lid and reduce the heat. Let them simmer for about 15 minutes or until soft. Remove the fruit with a slotted spoon and share between two bowls. Add a dollop of Greek yoghurt to each serving and drizzle a little of the cooking juices over the top. Serve immediately.

ITALIAN RAREBIT
with Oregano

SERVES: **2**
COOKING TIME: **20 MINUTES**

A small knob of butter | 2 tsp plain flour | 100ml milk
75g Taleggio or other creamy Italian cheese, roughly chopped | 1 egg yolk
1 tbsp chopped oregano | 2 slices of good white bread | 2 slices prosciutto
A handful of cherry tomatoes (optional)

This is like a cross between a Welsh Rarebit and the Croque Monsieur – cheese, ham, toast and grilled gooeyness. I've used all Italian ingredients (except the bread, because nothing beats a bit of Farmhouse White), but if you don't have them to hand you could just use regular ham or cheese. Rich, filling and satisfying, this is a hangover cure at its most perfect.

Preheat the grill to high. Melt the butter in a small pan. Stir in the flour to form a thick, smooth paste. Gradually add the milk, a little at a time, stirring constantly until you have a creamy sauce. Add the cheese, egg yolk and oregano and gently beat until the cheese has melted. The sauce should be a thick, gloopy consistency.

Toast the bread until golden brown on both sides. Place a slice of prosciutto on each piece of toast and spoon the cheese sauce on top. If you're using cherry tomatoes, cut them in half and dot them over the cheese.

Transfer the toast to a baking tray, cheese side up, and place them under the grill for 6–8 minutes, until the cheese is brown and bubbling. Serve immediately.

Substitute the oregano with...
BASIL, THYME, SAGE

BAKED EGGS
with Sage

SERVES: **2**
COOKING TIME: **20-25 MINUTES**

---

2 tbsp olive oil | 1 garlic clove, peeled and finely chopped | ½ tsp dried chilli flakes
½ tsp cayenne pepper | 1 tsp paprika | 1½ tbsp chopped sage leaves, plus leaves to decorate
1 red pepper | 400g tin of chopped tomatoes | 2 slices of good bread, for serving | 4 eggs
A little butter, for spreading | 2 tbsp crème fraîche

I first had a variant of this dish at Ottolenghi's brilliant London restaurant Nopi. Called Shakshuka, it was, as you'd expect, all Middle Eastern spices and exotic dollops of yoghurt, combining to create a wonderful – if deceptively simple – brunch. I gave up trying to create a replica of his version and instead devised this, the sage being less of a nod to foreign climes, but just as delicious. And I reckon this recipe is probably far easier to create at home. Serve on a lazy Saturday morning, with the weekend papers to hand, and nothing but a late lunch on the agenda.

Add the oil to a medium-sized saucepan with a lid, and set it over a fairly high heat. Once it begins to get hot, add the garlic, chilli, cayenne pepper, paprika and sage and cover for 3–4 minutes. Wash, chop and deseed the pepper and add it to the pan. Give everything a stir and cover it for another 3–4 minutes, or until the pepper is soft.

Pour in the tomatoes, reduce the heat and let everything simmer away for 8–10 minutes, until the mixture has reduced to a nicely thick and sticky consistency.

This is the part where timing is key – you are probably going to want to pop the bread into the toaster just before you add the eggs to the saucepan. Break the eggs on top of the tomato mixture, evenly spaced around the pan and as quickly as possible. Cover the pan again and let them poach for 2–3 minutes – long enough for the whites to look solid but not so long that the yolks go hard. Sprinkle over a few whole sage leaves to garnish.

Butter the toast, place each slice on a plate and, using a large fish slice, carefully divide the baked eggs and tomatoes between the slices of toast, taking care not to break the yolks of the eggs. Top each with a large dollop of crème fraîche and serve immediately.

Substitute the
sage with...
OREGANO, BASIL,
TARRAGON

Starters & Sides

I was never very good at dinner parties.
Like a pungent white goats cheese,
I crumble under pressure. The guests will
be arriving and I'll be chopping, peeling,
sweating and hissing furtive commands
at my boyfriend.

But I've discovered the secret. And it's not
groundbreaking or anything to stress about.
It's to let the ingredients do the work so that
you have more time to entertain your guests.
I used to think it was the more complex
dishes that were the most impressive, but if
you match a couple of unusual flavours and
keep everyone's glasses topped up, they'll be
far more likely to have a good time.

All the following suggestions centre
around the idea of snipping a handful of
herbs from their boxes and throwing them
together with a few other ingredients. Many
can be prepared the night before, which
will give the impression that you're a natural
host. Simple, quick and delicious, as easy –
if not even more so – as pie.

*Substitute
the dill with...*
MINT, BASIL, OREGANO

Dill and
ROASTED RED PEPPER DIP

SERVES: **4**
COOKING TIME: **30 MINUTES**

2 red peppers, plus extra raw and diced for serving | Olive oil
100g walnuts, roughly chopped
4 tbsp soured cream | 2 tbsp tomato purée
Juice of 1 lemon | 4 sprigs of dill, chopped, plus extra for serving

I always think it's important to put snacks out for guests when they first arrive; otherwise they tend to drink too much and end up not being able to enjoy the real starter. Or is that just my friends? This creamy dip is light but satisfying – feel free to add a few drops of Tabasco sauce if you like a bit of a kick.

Preheat the oven to 200°C/Gas mark 6. Rinse the peppers and brush them with a little olive oil. Place the whole peppers in a small roasting tray and drizzle a splash more oil over the top. Roast the peppers for 15 minutes and then add the walnut pieces, basting them in the oil and roasting everything for another 15 minutes. Set aside to cool.

Once the peppers are cool enough to handle, peel the skin off and discard, cut them in half lengthways, remove the stalks and scrape out the seeds. Take the flesh in your hand and give it a really good squeeze over the sink – quite a bit of liquid will run out through your fingers. Put the squidged peppers into a blender with all but a tablespoon of the walnuts and blitz.

Add the soured cream, tomato purée and lemon juice and blitz again until you have a smooth paste. Stir the dill into the mixture by hand.

Divide the dip between two bowls and sprinkle over the remaining walnut pieces, diced red pepper and a little extra dill. This works well served with toast, strips of pitta bread and sticks of cucumber.

BRAISED BROAD BEANS
with Mint

SERVES: **4-6**
COOKING TIME: **30 MINUTES**

25g butter | 1 tbsp plain flour | 285ml vegetable stock
500g frozen broad beans | Salt | Juice of ½ lemon
3 tbsp chopped mint leaves | 1 slice of sourdough bread per person
Pecorino shavings, for serving

This is one of those simple starters that is packed full of so much flavour it doesn't matter that there are barely any ingredients. The beans are softened to buttery perfection – so much so that you don't need to peel them – and the mint leaves add a hit of summer garden goodness. In fact, the first time I made it my friend Katy complained that she thought the cheese was too much, as the veg really didn't need it. I've kept it in because I think most dishes are improved with the addition of cheese, but use it sparingly, or not at all.

Melt the butter in a saucepan with a lid over a medium heat and add the flour, stirring them together to form a smooth paste. Gradually add the stock, a little at a time, until you have a rich, smooth sauce.

Add the broad beans, a pinch of salt, the lemon juice and mint. Cover and let simmer gently for 25 minutes, or until the broad beans are tender.

Meanwhile, toast the bread and divide it between your plates. Spoon a generous heap of beans onto each slice, top with a few shavings of Pecorino and serve.

Substitute the mint with...
CHERVIL, BASIL,
LEMON BALM

Substitute the
calendula with...
BASIL, OREGANO,
NASTURTIUM

Celery, Stilton and Calendula
SOUP

SERVES: **4**
COOKING TIME: **40-45 MINUTES**

100g butter | 200g celery, roughly chopped
1 onion, peeled and chopped | 1 litre vegetable stock
100ml double cream | 100g Stilton
2 tbsp chopped calendula flowers, plus extra for serving

This recipe is everything you want a soup to be – creamy, salty, rich, buttery and, most importantly, easy to make. Calendula flowers (more commonly known as marigold) have a peppery taste, so they help to balance the seasoning. If you're using any of the herb substitutions opposite, add a grind of black pepper too.

Melt the butter in a large saucepan with a lid over a low heat. Add the celery and onion and let them sweat, with the lid on, for 10 minutes.

Add the stock and let simmer gently for 30 minutes, placing the lid on at an angle to allow the steam to escape. Once cooked through, use a stick blender to purée it all into a smooth liquid.

Pour in the cream, crumble in the Stilton and add the calendula. Stir the soup until the cheese has melted but don't let it boil. Serve immediately with a couple of extra calendula flowers placed artfully on the top of each bowl.

Prawn, Coriander and Rose
COCKTAIL

SERVES: **4**
PREPARATION TIME: **10 MINUTES**

100g crunchy lettuce, such as cos, torn | 300g watermelon, peeled and cubed
Rose water | 200g Atlantic prawns, cooked and peeled
4 tbsp chopped coriander | Rose petals, for serving (optional)

Prawn Cocktail, that staple of 1980s' cuisine, has been given a bad name thanks largely to the cloying pink sauce that usually came with it. If you strip the ingredients back to their basics, they're actually very fresh, modern and, dare I say it, gently ironic. This light starter is ideal on hot summer nights, or when you really don't want to make a fuss.

Divide the lettuce between four bowls, then scatter over the watermelon cubes. With a very steady hand, sprinkle one large drop of rose water onto the watermelon – in each bowl one small drop isn't quite enough but two will be too many.

Divide the prawns, coriander and rose petals, if using, between the bowls. Serve immediately or pop in the fridge for an hour or so until your guests arrive.

Substitute the coriander with...
MINT, BASIL,
LEMON BALM

Cucumber, Borage and
SALMON SALAD

———●———

SERVES: **4**
PREPARATION TIME: **10 MINUTES**

———●———

1 cucumber | 3 spring onions, chopped | 1 little gem lettuce, torn
2 cooked salmon fillets, flaked | Juice of 1 lime
2 tbsp olive oil | 2 tbsp chopped borage flowers

Borage is another of those old herbs that seems to have fallen out of fashion, despite it's refreshing, "cucumbery" taste and its ability to go really well in a Pimm's. It's almost too easy to grow, taking over pots at an alarming rate, but it goes well in almost any salad. This light summery dish can be made in advance and kept in the fridge until needed. You can serve this with a jacket potato if you fancy something more substantial.

Chop the cucumber into rounds about 2cm thick, then cut them into quarters. Transfer to a serving bowl with the spring onions, lettuce and salmon.

In a jar, shake together the lime juice and olive oil, and pour it over the salad. Sprinkle over the borage flowers and serve.

Substitute the borage with...
DILL, MINT, CHERVIL

ARTICHOKES
with Nasturtium Butter

SERVES: **4**
COOKING TIME: **25-30 MINUTES**

---

4 artichokes | Olive oil | 2 garlic cloves, peeled and chopped
2 tbsp nasturtium petals, finely chopped | 100g salted butter
Juice of 1 lemon | Salt

They may look pretty and sweet but nasturtiums have the peppery undertones of a radish, and are more savoury than their sun-filled petals imply. This is finger food at its most impressive… and messiest. The perfect dinner party icebreaker, it's impossible to keep formalities going whilst slurping the buttery meat from each leaf. Serve with plenty of napkins, bowls for discarded artichoke bits and a nudge of gentle encouragement for guests to get stuck in.

Cut the stalks off the artichokes, pull away the outer leaves and trim the top 2cm or so with a very sharp knife. Place the trimmed bulbs in a steamer over boiling water and cook for 25–30 minutes, or until you are able to easily pierce the base with a sharp knife.

Meanwhile, heat a splash of oil in a small pan over a medium heat and add the garlic, allowing it to gently sizzle to a golden colour. Add the nasturtium, butter, lemon juice and a sprinkling of salt and cook for a few minutes or until it all becomes a rich, molten liquor.

Once the artichokes are cooked, place them into individual bowls and drizzle the butter mixture evenly amongst them. Serve immediately, showing your guests how to pull off each leaf and suck the artichoke meat out of the base. Keep a few finger bowls and napkins tactfully at the ready.

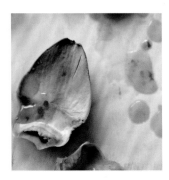

Substitute the
nasturtiums with...
THYME, ROSEMARY,
SUMMER SAVORY

Chive Flower
PIZZETTA

—————— ● ——————

SERVES: **4-6**
COOKING TIME: **10-12 MINUTES**

—————— ● ——————

1 baguette | Olive oil
50g salted butter, at room temperature | Salt
2 chive flowers, petals only, plus extra for decorating
Toppings of your choice – see below for suggestions

Not taking any of the effort that making a pizza requires, this pizzetta is like a glorified garlic bread, but oh, how glorified it is! It's delicious with melted cheese dripping over the side, but you can get creative with your toppings as pretty much any flavours will work here.

Slice the baguette in half lengthways and lay the halves, cut-side up, on a baking tray. You may need to cut them into shorter lengths to get them to fit on the tray, but try to keep the bread as big as possible.

Douse the bread in olive oil, covering it right to the edges, as it will seep through and moisten what will become your pizzetta base. Leave it to soak up all the oil and get a bit soggy. Meanwhile mix together the butter, a generous pinch of salt and chive petals. Spread the butter mixture liberally over the top of the bread.

This will be delicious on its own, but you can add any extra topping you might fancy at this point. Ham and olive; mushroom and Grana Padano; tomato purée and cheddar, all work well, but do steer clear of using onion and garlic, as the chive petals have a strong enough flavour already.

Place the pizzetta in the oven for 10–12 minutes until the sides of the bread start to look a little crispy. Cut into portions – from bite-size chunks to 10cm lengths – and sprinkle some more chive flowers over the top. Serve immediately.

Substitute the
chive flowers with...
BASIL, OREGANO,
NASTURTIUM

Chilli and Rosemary
CARROT SPEARS

SERVES: **6**
COOKING TIME: **25 MINUTES**

3 tbsp olive oil | 400g carrots, trimmed and peeled
2 stalks of rosemary, leaves only | Salt
Chilli oil, for serving | Grated Parmesan, for serving

This is finger food at its least sophisticated but most enjoyable. The host doesn't have to fiddle around stuffing vol-au-vents and the guests can feel happy in the knowledge that they are being a bit healthy whilst devouring the satisfyingly delicious cheese and chilli combo. This is best served as an appetiser before people sit down – it is unusual and requires not much more work than turning out a bag of crisps – but it can also be served as a side dish.

Preheat the oven to 200°C/Gas mark 6. Tip the oil into a roasting tray and place it in the oven. Meanwhile, slice the carrots in half lengthways. Slice each in half lengthways again so that every carrot is cut into four spears. Place the carrots in the roasting tray of hot oil and add the rosemary leaves and a good pinch of salt. Carefully mix everything together so that the carrots are well basted and place the tray back in the oven for 25 minutes, or until the carrots are looking a bit crispy and roasted.

Transfer the carrots to a platter using a slotted spoon, bringing with them the bits of rosemary but leaving behind as much of the oil as possible. Drizzle them with a little chilli oil and throw a nice big handful of grated Parmesan over the top. Serve immediately.

Substitute the
rosemary with...
THYME, SAGE,
MARJORAM

Light Dishes

Some of these dishes are quick lunches that you can eat on the go, others are simple fuss-free dinners that focus more on feeling fresh than on filling you up. Every single one of them can be eaten at any time of year, but their focus is on sunshine flavours, nourishing you with a lightness that evokes those sunny Saturdays spent eating outside with your friends.

These delicious recipes are inspired by the dream of what life should be like – lazy and relaxed summer days filled with food and drink – re-imagined for what life really is – busy, complicated and often hectic.

Sorrel and
BUTTERED CEPS

———— • ————

SERVES: **1**
COOKING TIME: **5 MINUTES**

———— • ————

50g salted butter, plus extra for spreading | 75g ceps, cleaned and sliced
2 tbsp chopped sorrel, plus extra for serving | 1 garlic clove, peeled and chopped
1 egg | 1 slice of thick bread

This is my favourite Saturday lunch, following a trip to the market to buy dirty, earth-covered ceps and freshly baked bread (it's advisable to give the ceps a very thorough wipe or wash as you never know what you'll find). This goes particularly well with a crisp, very cold glass of chenin blanc or Chablis, which will cut through the richness of the runny yolk. Indulgent yet ready in minutes.

Melt the butter in a small frying pan and toss in the ceps, sorrel and garlic. Lightly fry everything, stirring regularly, for 5 minutes.

Meanwhile, poach the egg. I use an egg poacher, and steam it for exactly 2½ minutes to get a runny yolk, but if you don't have this piece of kit then simply pour boiling water into a pan, to a depth of about 2cm, and set it over a high heat. Crack the egg into a ladle, carefully rest the ladle in the pan and make sure the water doesn't come over the top of it. Cover the pan, leaving just a crack where the ladle's handle juts out. Poach for 2½ minutes.

Meanwhile, toast the bread until golden, butter and transfer to a serving plate. Cover with the mushroom mixture and once the egg is cooked, place it on top of the mushrooms, scatter over a little more chopped sorrel and serve immediately.

Substitute the sorrel with...
CHIVES, THYME, TARRAGON

Substitute the rosemary with...
THYME, CALENDULA, MARJORAM

Rosemary, Red Grape and
GOAT'S CHEESE QUINOA

SERVES: **2**
COOKING TIME: **15-20 MINUTES**

100g quinoa | Olive oil | 1 sprig of rosemary, leaves only
200ml apple juice | 100g red grapes, halved | 2 celery stalks, chopped
100g hard goat's cheese such as Inglewhite, crumbled

Quinoa gets a bad rap, but that's only because it looks boring and self-righteous. Yet infused here with the apple and rosemary and served with crunchy fresh ingredients it becomes nutty, almost creamy, and somehow slightly indulgent. Eat right away or store in an air-tight container in the fridge for lunch at your desk – this is satisfyingly good-for-you fast food.

Rinse the quinoa well, then place in a saucepan with a drizzle of oil, the rosemary leaves, apple juice and 200ml of cold water. Bring to the boil, then simmer over a medium heat for 15–20 minutes until all the liquid is absorbed, giving it the occasional stir and keeping a watchful eye that it never boils dry. Add a splash more water if you think it looks like it needs it. Leave to cool.

Split the cold quinoa between two bowls and scatter over the grapes, celery and goat's cheese and serve.

Substitute the jasmine with...
LAVENDER, MINT, MARJORAM

RAINBOW CHARD SALAD
with a Jasmine Dressing

SERVES: **2**
COOKING TIME: **2-3 MINUTES**

250g rainbow chard | 200g pickled baby beetroot, roughly chopped
50g walnuts, chopped
For the dressing: 1 tsp lemon juice | 2 tsp ricotta
1½ tbsp olive oil | 1½ tbsp cider vinegar | 6–9 jasmine flowers | Salt

This very simple salad can be added to if you want to bulk it up, but I like the mix of textures – the crunchy walnuts contrast nicely with the soft chard. A bit of mild goat's cheese goes well crumbled over the top, but the gentle flavour of the jasmine dressing will be overpowered if you go with anything stronger. Some crusty buttered bread to mop up any leftover sauce could certainly be encouraged.

Wash the chard well and steam it in a steamer or in a heatproof colander set over a pan of boiling water for 2–3 minutes or until the stalks are soft. Remove it from the pan, divide it between two plates and let cool.

Scatter the beetroot and walnuts over the top of the chard. Put all the dressing ingredients into a jar, tighten the lid and shake together well. Pour it over the salad and serve.

Brie, Cranberry and Tarragon
STUFFED POTATO

SERVES: **1**
COOKING TIME: **60-75 MINUTES**

1 baking potato | 50g brie, cubed | 2 tsp cranberry sauce
1 tbsp chopped tarragon | Olive oil, for drizzling

When I told my mother-in-law I was writing a recipe book she said she hoped there were no stuffed mushrooms "or anything like that" because life is too short to fill a vegetable. I tend to agree, but with this dish it only takes seconds. There is a short cut of course – just bake the potato, slice it down the middle and shove the brie, cranberry and tarragon into the crack – but baking the brie makes it far runnier, gooier and more luxurious.

Preheat the oven to 200°C/Gas mark 6. Bake the potato until it is soft and fluffy in the centre. I give mine a 5 minute blast in the microwave to soften it a little before letting it crisp up in the oven for 25 minutes, but you could just place it in the oven and cook it for 45–60 minutes, depending on its size. Test it is done with a sharp knife.

Once cooked, halve the potato, scrape out the fluffy insides and mix them with all the remaining ingredients apart from the oil. Stuff the filling back into the potato skins, drizzle with a few drops of oil and return it to the oven for 15 minutes, or until the skin is really crispy. Serve with a crunchy salad and some cold meats.

Substitute the tarragon with...
ROSEMARY, CHIVE, BASIL

Posh Mackerel and Coriander
ON TOAST

SERVES: **1**
COOKING TIME: **10 MINUTES**

150g cherry tomatoes, halved | 1 tbsp olive oil | Black pepper | 1 tsp balsamic vinegar
1 smoked mackerel fillet, flaked | 1 tbsp chopped coriander
1 slice of granary bread, for serving | Butter, for spreading

On testing this recipe I bought twice as many ingredients as I'd need, just in case. This turned out to be lucky, as I wolfed the first plate down in seconds and quickly made the same again. It has been my go-to speedy lunch and get-home-late dinner ever since. The tomatoes taste fresh and syrupy and the fish is salty and rich. There really is nothing much to it, almost embarrassingly simple.

Place the tomatoes in a small saucepan with the oil and a really good grind of black pepper. Set the pan over a low heat and stir occasionally, letting the tomatoes fry for about 5 minutes.

Once the tomatoes start to split open, add the balsamic vinegar and turn the heat up, allowing everything to bubble for 2–3 minutes until it all looks like a nice thick sauce. Chuck the mackerel into the pan with the coriander, stirring everything together for 1 minute. Meanwhile, toast and butter the bread.

Spoon the tomato and mackerel mixture on top of the hot buttered toast and eat immediately.

Substitute the coriander with...
OREGANO, BASIL, SAGE

Honey and Lilac Topped
SEA BASS STEAKS

SERVES: **2**
COOKING TIME: **15-20 MINUTES**

4 tbsp olive oil, plus extra for greasing | 2 sea bass fillets | 4 tsp runny honey
50g pine nuts | Salt | 2 garlic cloves, peeled
1 tbsp chopped lilac flowers, plus extra for serving

Lilac doesn't taste quite as floral as it smells – it's not like rose and violet, which taste exactly the same as their fragrance. It's ever so slightly bitter, with a saltiness that works well with the fish. This easy topping should cling nicely to the fish, but any that falls off onto the tray makes for a nice bit of extra crunch.

Preheat the oven to 180°C/Gas mark 4. Line a baking tray with foil and grease with a little oil. Place the sea bass fillets on the tray, skin side down. Mix together the oil and the honey and use half of the mixture to glaze the fish. Set the other half aside for later.

In a blender, blitz together the rest of the ingredients with the remaining oil and honey mixture. Spread this chunky paste over the fish and bake in the oven for 15–20 minutes or until the paste looks golden, crunchy and a little, for want of a better word, crusty. Serve the fish with a little extra lilac over the top, a green salad and some new potatoes.

Substitute the
lilac with...
ROSEMARY,
NASTURTIUM, THYME

Pea, Purslane and PANSY SALAD

• ---

SERVES: **2-4**
COOKING TIME: **15-20 MINUTES**

• ---

125g jasmine rice | 75g fresh peas, podded
1 ripe mango, peeled, stone removed and diced
1 bunch of purslane | 50g Atlantic prawns, cooked and peeled
2 tbsp chopped basil, plus whole leaves for serving
Juice of 1 lemon | 1 tbsp olive oil | Pansies, for serving

Purslane is much maligned – despite being a staple in the Middle East it is considered a weed in the States. It's a shame because I always like seeing it on menus, its salty bite adding a savoury depth to every salad and sauce. This big sharing bowl would go well with a platter of cold meats and pies, the bright colours of the herbs, fruit and flowers sitting prettily on any plate.

Tip the rice into a saucepan with a lid and add 250ml of cold water. Set it over a medium heat and let it slowly come to the boil. Reduce the heat to a simmer, cover the pan and let it bubble away for 15–20 minutes or until all the water has been absorbed. Turn the rice out into a sieve and jiggle it about under a cold tap to let all the starch rinse away.

Transfer the rice to a large serving bowl and mix in the peas, mango, purslane, prawns and basil. Shake the lemon juice and oil together in a jar and pour over the salad, tossing everything together well. Scatter some pansies over the top and serve.

Substitute the
purslane with...
BASIL, MINT,
OREGANO

Lemon Balm and Parsley
SPAGHETTI

SERVES: **2**
COOKING TIME: **15 MINUTES**

Olive oil | 100g spaghetti | 2 garlic cloves, peeled and chopped
1 tsp dried chilli flakes | 1 courgette | Juice of 1 lemon
2 stalks of lemon balm, leaves only
1 tbsp chopped parsley | Grated Parmesan, for serving (optional)

Pinching lemon balm between my fingers is one of my earliest childhood memories. Running through the garden, I would stop and marvel at how something that looked so unassuming could smell so fresh, a hint of Mediterranean exoticism hidden in a suburban herb border. We never did anything with it – although my mother once tried to make a tea with the fresh leaves which was apparently "pretty potent". It's a shame because it actually adds a very pleasant zing – the lemon flavour you'd expect and a slight savoury undertone. Use it instead of lemon zest in cakes, to make lemon drinks (don't be put off by my mum's failed experiment) or in this very peppy pasta.

Add a splash of olive oil to a large pan of water and bring to the boil. Once bubbling, add the spaghetti and cook according to the packet instructions.

Meanwhile, add a glug of oil to another saucepan with a lid, and set over a medium heat. Once warm, add the garlic and chilli and cover, letting them sweat for 2–3 minutes until the garlic is a golden brown. Trim and slice the courgette in half lengthways and then chop into slices about 1cm thick. Add the courgette to the pan of garlic, stir, cover and cook for about 5 minutes, until the courgette is soft and beginning to brown.

Remove the courgette pan from the heat and stir in the lemon juice – it will splutter – and return to the heat to cook off some of the liquid.

Drain the pasta once it is cooked and add it to the courgette pan with the leaves from the lemon balm. Stir everything together; place the pan back on the heat if you feel it needs another minute to warm through.

Divide the spaghetti mixture between two bowls, sprinkle over the parsley and some Parmesan if you like. Eat immediately.

Substitute the
lemon balm and
parsley with...
MINT AND BASIL, LEMON
THYME AND OREGANO,
NASTURTIUM AND THYME

Cheesy Bacon, Spinach and
CHIVE WRAP

SERVES: **1**
COOKING TIME: **6 MINUTES**

---

2 rashers of bacon, rind left on and chopped | 1 flour tortilla wrap
50g baby spinach leaves | 50g Stilton, crumbled
1 tbsp chopped chives | 4–5 cherry tomatoes, halved

All warm, comforting and yet with a slight nod to a healthy lunch (well, it has some veg in it!), there are quite a lot of strong flavours at work here – the saltiness of the bacon and Stilton, the pungent chives and the sheer deliciousness of all three together. The spinach acts as a blotting paper to soak them all up and stop them from becoming too much to handle. It works equally well with a mild cheddar.

Set a frying pan over a high heat and once it's hot add the bacon, stirring it around for 5 minutes so that it starts to brown and become crispy. Spread the wrap out on a plate and tip the bacon and any fat it has emitted into the middle. Set aside to allow the flavours to soak in.

Return the pan to the heat and throw in the spinach, Stilton and chives, stirring continuously for 1 minute. The Stilton will melt and the leaves will begin to wilt – tip the mixture over the bacon and place the cherry tomatoes on top. Carefully fold the wrap up from the bottom and over at the sides so that it creates a pocket you can easily hold. Eat immediately.

Substitute the chive with...
BASIL, SAGE, OREGANO

Herby Turkey and Parsnip
MASH PIES

SERVES: **4**
COOKING TIME: **35-40 MINUTES**

100g butter, plus a little extra | 400g turkey breast, chopped into chunks
100g frozen peas | Salt | 1 tbsp plain flour | 4 tbsp soured cream
2 tbsp chopped basil | 1 tbsp chopped mint
400g parsnips, peeled | Black pepper

Admittedly these are quite filling, so you could happily make the whole lot in one pie dish and serve it as dinner for two. Parsnip mash isn't quite as heavy as potato, and because there is no cheese it's lighter than it sounds.

Preheat the oven to 180°C/Gas mark 4. Melt the butter in a large saucepan over a medium heat and add the turkey, frozen peas and a pinch of salt. Cook for 5–10 minutes, stirring occasionally, until the peas have defrosted, the turkey is lightly golden and the butter is bubbling. Add the flour and stir until dissolved. Mix in the soured cream, basil and mint and set aside for later.

Meanwhile, slice the parsnips into rounds. Transfer to a pan of boiling water and cook for 15 minutes until soft and they can easily be pierced with a sharp knife. Drain well, return the parsnip to the empty pan and cook over a medium heat for a couple of seconds to let any remaining water evaporate. Add a knob of butter and a little pepper and mash until smooth.

Split the turkey mixture between four individual mini pie or casserole dishes – each one should be able to hold about 250ml. Cover each with a quarter of the mash, smoothing it down carefully. Place in the oven for 20 minutes, serving once the filling is bubbling gently up the sides.

Substitute the basil and mint with...
CHIVE AND TARRAGON,
ROSEMARY AND THYME,
LEMON THYME AND
PARSLEY

Main Dishes

There are two types of main course. One is quick and simple, cooked just for you and your family and thrown together in a few minutes with ingredients picked up in a dash to the shops. The other is more involved, the central point of a dinner party, the exact moment in the evening where everyone has relaxed but nobody has quite drunk themselves under the table yet. The conduit to an atmosphere of delighted goodwill.

And both types can be elevated with a couple of sprigs from the garden. Whatever the occasion, none of these dishes require very much preparation – you've done the hard work by growing the herbs and flowers in the first place, or by setting the table, or by simply coordinating all your friends' diaries so that you're in the same place at the same time. Cooking dinner should be a relaxing start to an enjoyable evening, which all of these recipes ensure that it will be.

Summer Roast Chicken
WITH PEACHES AND BASIL

SERVES: **6**
COOKING TIME: **1 HOUR 20 MINUTES**

1.3kg chicken | 250ml white wine | 4–5 sprigs of thyme
1kg new potatoes | 100ml oil | Salt
3 peaches, stones removed and sliced
3 tbsp chopped basil, plus extra for serving

Boiling the chicken before roasting it sounds like a bit of an effort, but it really is worth it. It ensures that the meat is juicy, tender and truly delicious. As for the peaches, they turn into a bit of a purée and act as an instant chutney that is as fragrant as it is tasty – a fresh and light way to do Sunday lunch.

Preheat the oven to 220°C/Gas mark 7. Place the chicken breast side down in a large saucepan. Add the wine, thyme and enough cold water to completely cover the bird. Bring to the boil and leave for 10 minutes. In a separate large saucepan, boil the potatoes for 10 minutes.

Meanwhile, add the oil to a large roasting tin and place it in the oven to heat up. Once the chicken has boiled for 10 minutes, carefully remove it from the liquid (which can be kept as an excellent stock) and place it breast side up in the roasting tin. Drain the potatoes and slowly place them in around the sides of the chicken (be careful as the oil will spit). Spoon the sizzling oil over the potatoes and chicken to cover. Sprinkle a good pinch of salt over the whole lot.

Put the tin back in the oven and let it cook for 30 minutes before lowering the temperature to 170°C/Gas mark 3, basting everything with the juices and oil. Cook for another 30 minutes before checking the juices run clear when a knife is inserted into the thickest part of the bird. If they don't, return to the oven for 10 minutes before testing again. If they do, remove the chicken from the dish, sit it on a plate, cover in foil and rest for up to 10 minutes. Add the peaches and basil to the potatoes, give them a good stir and return the dish to the oven for another 10 minutes.

Carve the chicken and serve it with spoonfuls of the potatoes and peaches. Drizzle over a little juice from the tin and sprinkle with some fresh basil. Serve with some green veg.

Substitute the
basil with...
MINT, THYME,
TARRAGON

Substitute the chives with...
TARRAGON, PARSLEY, OREGANO

CHEESY HAM AND CHIVE
"Shepherd's Pie"

●

SERVES: **4**
COOKING TIME: **45-50 MINUTES**

●

200g thickly sliced ham, torn into large chunks | 50ml hot vegetable stock
150ml double cream | Juice of ½ lemon | 1 tbsp Dijon mustard
2 tbsp chopped chives | 100g mature cheddar cheese, grated, plus extra for the topping
Black pepper | 600g potatoes | Butter

It seems odd that creamy mashed potato toppings have for so long been kept solely for lamb, beef and fish. As soon as the idea of chicken, mushroom and tarragon under mash is suggested, it's very why-didn't-I-think-of-that-before-ness hits you with some force. Similarly, ham and chive works equally well, the potent onion flavours of the chive cutting through the rich sauce. Don't be tempted to add any salt – it really doesn't need it. There isn't much to this dish, which makes its potato and cheesy goodness all the more heartening.

Scatter the ham around the base of a shallow pie dish. If you are using a stock cube to make the stock, only crumble in about ½ of the cube or its saltiness will overpower the dish. In a large bowl, mix the hot stock with all the remaining ingredients apart from the potatoes and butter. Season with some black pepper. Pour the mixture over the ham, spreading it all out evenly.

Preheat the oven to 180°C/Gas mark 4. Peel, halve and boil the potatoes for about 20 minutes, until a knife slices through them easily. Once cooked, drain and mash with a knob of butter. Spoon the potatoes over the creamy ham mixture and carefully smooth with the back of a spoon. Sprinkle some extra cheese over the top and bake for 25–30 minutes, until golden and bubbling, and the cheese has started to brown. Serve with peas, carrots or a crisp green salad.

Lemon and Chervil
POACHED SALMON

SERVES: **2**
COOKING TIME: **10 MINUTES**

2 salmon fillets | 2 heaped tsp salt | 1 tbsp oil
1 tbsp chopped chervil | Juice of 1 lemon | 150g crème fraîche
Borage or mint flowers, for serving (optional)

My partner's grandmother – aged 92 – has always cooked fish in this way, which explains its old-fashioned, Mrs Beetonesque salt water method. It feels very counterintuitive, but the fish turns out perfectly every time, tender and wonderfully flavourful. The lemon and chervil make a tangy accompaniment – this is the sort of meal you can serve when you've got home from work and can't face any real cooking. Easy, but impressive.

Place the salmon fillets into a saucepan with a lid and cover the fish completely with cold water, adding in the salt. Two heaped teaspoons feels a lot but don't worry, you won't taste it, it just means that the boiling point of the water is raised. Cover and set over a very low heat, keeping a close eye on it.

Meanwhile, add the oil to a frying pan set over a fairly high heat and cook the chervil for a couple of minutes, until it sizzles and starts to smell quite fragrant. Add the lemon juice and crème fraiche and stir everything together on the hob, removing it from the heat before it boils. At this point, the cold water around the fish should be getting close to a small boil – the moment the water starts to move (about 10 minutes after you set it on the heat), the salmon is cooked and should be immediately removed from the pan using a slotted spoon.

Serve the fish straightaway, with the lemon sauce drizzled liberally over the top. Scatter with a few borage or mint flowers if you have them and serve with some boiled potatoes, mash or peas on the side.

Substitute the
chervil with...
DILL, MINT,
LEMON BALM

Clockwise: Various; dried flowers; lavender

Oregano and
FENNEL GRATIN

---•---

SERVES: **2**
Cooking time: **35-40 MINUTES**

---•---

1 fennel bulb | 3 spring onions, chopped
25g butter | 2 tbsp flour | 350ml milk
2 tbsp chopped oregano | 100g mature cheddar cheese, grated
2 slices of white bread, crusts removed

I had planned this dish to be made with sage, but the gently aromatic flavour of the fennel was overpowered with the herb's robust strength. For something this filled with cheese, it tasted really bad. Oregano on the other hand was an unexpected delight – its subtle Italian hint working with and not against the fennel. Creamy, rich and delicately delicious.

Preheat the oven to 180°C/Gas mark 4. Wash the fennel and trim off its base and head. Quarter it and place it in a steamer over boiling water for 6–7 minutes until soft. Remove from the steamer and transfer to a roasting dish. Scatter the spring onions over and around them.

Melt the butter in a saucepan over a medium heat, add the flour and whisk together to make a thick, smooth paste. Gradually add the milk a little at a time, while constantly stirring, until you have a beautiful pale and glossy sauce. Add the oregano and most of the cheese, stirring to stop the sauce from catching on the bottom, and bring it to a very slow boil. As soon as it starts to bubble, pour the sauce over the fennel and spring onions.

Blitz the bread in a food processor to make breadcrumbs and sprinkle them over the top of the cheesy fennel along with the last of the grated cheese. Place the dish in the oven for 20 minutes – you may wish to finish it off with 5 minutes under the grill if you don't think it's brown enough on top. Serve with a green salad and crusty bread.

Substitute the oregano with...
BASIL, CHIVE,
TARRAGON

Chicken and
CORIANDER DAUBE

SERVES: **4-6**
COOKING TIME: **2 HOURS**

Plain flour | Salt | 8 boneless chicken thighs
2 tbsp olive oil | 1 onion, peeled and chopped | 150g mushrooms, chopped
3 celery stalks, chopped | 50g tinned anchovies, in olive oil | 3 tbsp brandy
600ml chicken stock | A large handful of coriander
Pomegranate seeds, for serving (optional)

Daube is just a French word for stew – usually one that is made with very inexpensive meat. Here the flavours are much greater than the sum of their parts, the brandy giving the sauce a real richness, whilst the coriander and celery add a nice bit of bite. I like to serve this with pomegranate seeds, but they're not essential – they look pretty and they help to make the dish not feel too heavy, but it can certainly survive without.

Substitute the coriander with...
THYME, BASIL, TARRAGON

Cover a plate with a good amount of flour and season with a little salt. Dip each chicken thigh into the seasoned flour so that they're well covered. In a large ovenproof pan with a lid, heat the oil over a medium heat and once hot, add the chicken and keep turning to brown on all sides – you will probably need to do these in batches, with each taking about 2–3 minutes. Once browned, remove the chicken from the pan and set aside for later.

Add the onion, mushrooms and celery to the empty pan with a little bit more oil if you think that it needs it. Season with a pinch of salt and let them sweat gently for 5 minutes so that they are soft but not too coloured. Once soft, fish them out with a slotted spoon and set them aside with the meat.

Preheat the oven to 180°C/Gas mark 4. Place the anchovies and all of their oil into the empty pan and add the brandy. Over a medium heat let it all bubble away, scraping the bottom to deglaze the pan until the anchovies dissolve and become a thick goo and the alcohol has burnt off. Return the chicken and vegetables to the pan, add the stock and bring everything to the boil.

Cover the pan with the lid and cook in the oven for 1 hour 20 minutes. After this time, remove the pan from the oven, add the coriander and give it all a really good stir. Place it back in the oven for 10 minutes. Serve with rice, potatoes or greens, and with the pomegranate seeds scattered over if you like.

Leek, Mushroom and
TARRAGON "QUICHE"

SERVES: **4**
COOKING TIME: **1 HOUR 5 MINUTES**

25g butter | 150g mushrooms, chopped
1 large leek, chopped | Black pepper | 3 eggs
150ml double cream | 2 sprigs of tarragon, broken up
75g cheddar cheese, grated

I use the term "quiche" very loosely as this actually doesn't have a pastry base – it's just the filling in all its rich and gooey glory. If it wasn't for all the cream and cheese you could almost call this a lighter alternative, but the amount of dairy puts paid to that. Still, it's ever so tasty, and that's all that really counts.

Preheat the oven to 160°C/Gas mark 3. Melt the butter in a large saucepan over a low heat and add the mushrooms and the leek, sautéing for 5 minutes until soft and just starting to brown. Pour into a deep, heat-resistant glass roasting dish and season with black pepper.

In a bowl, beat together the rest of the ingredients until well combined using a fork and spoon the liquid mixture over the vegetables. Place the dish in the oven for 1 hour until set and slightly brown on top. Slice it into quarters and serve with a green salad – I find it also goes particularly well with coleslaw.

Substitute the
tarragon with...
BASIL, CHERVIL,
OREGANO

Substitute the mustard flowers with...
THYME, NASTURTIUM, WINTER SAVORY

Barley and Mustard Flower
BEEF SOUP

SERVES: **4**
COOKING TIME: **1 HOUR 10 MINUTES**

2 tbsp plain flour | Salt | Black pepper | 500g frying steak, cubed
2 tbsp olive oil | 2 carrots, peeled and chopped
2 celery stalks, chopped | 100g mushrooms, chopped
3 spring onions, chopped | 2 kaffir lime leaves, chopped
2 tbsp mustard flowers, plus extra for decoration | 250ml red wine
500ml beef stock | 75g pearl barley

Warming barley stew is a winter favourite of mine, and this hearty beef version will cheer you on even the coldest of days. The mustard adds a little heat, and the kaffir lime adds a citrus tang, stopping it from feeling too stodgy. It keeps beautifully in an airtight container in the fridge, tasting even better when heated the next day, so make it in large batches and eat when you like.

Preheat the oven to 180°C/Gas mark 4. Place the flour in a bowl and add some seasoning. Toss the cubes of steak in the flour to cover. Heat the oil in a large ovenproof pan with a lid over a high heat and fry the steak in batches, removing it from the pan with a slotted spoon once it's brown on all its edges. Set the meat aside.

If the pan is a little dry add some more oil and turn the heat down to medium. Throw all the vegetables, lime leaves and mustard flowers into the pan and cover with a lid. Leave them to sauté together nicely for about 10 minutes, or until soft. Return the meat to the pan, add the red wine and let the wine come to the boil, mixing all the ingredients together.

Add the stock and barley, put the lid on and bring the soup to the boil. If it doesn't look very soup like and is quite thick, add some more stock. You don't want it to be thin, but there needs to be an element of liquor to the pan. Check the seasoning and then put the bubbling soup into the oven for 45 minutes.

Serve piping hot with some crusty bread and salted butter on the side.

Apricot, Thyme and
CHICKEN PIE

SERVES: **6-8**
COOKING TIME: **1 HOUR 5 MINUTES**

Flour, for dusting | 500g shortcrust pastry | 1 tbsp oil | 1 large leek, finely sliced
600g chicken breasts, roughly chopped | 2 tbsp chopped thyme
6 good-quality sausages | Salt | Black pepper | 150g dried apricots | Milk, for glazing

This is a modern take on a true classic – ploughman's tart. The pie is best when it is eaten cold and in nice thick slices. The apricots act a bit like chutney, so you don't need to worry about many condiments and the pie also works well with new potatoes, salad and plenty of mayonnaise.

Preheat the oven to 180°C/Gas mark 4. Dust your work surface with a little flour and roll the pastry out as thinly as you can. Use it to line a 30cm circular tin. Trim the excess from the sides and reserve any leftovers for later.

Heat the oil in a pan over a low heat and add the leek, stirring occasionally, for 5 minutes or until a soft golden colour.

Put the chicken and thyme into a large mixing bowl. Squeeze the sausage meat out of their skins and add to the bowl of chicken. It's messy, but kind of enjoyably so. Wash your hands and add a big pinch of salt and a couple of hearty grinds of pepper. Using a stick blender, blitz the meats together to form a very gooey paste. Once there are no large bits left, add the leeks and fold them in using a wooden spoon.

Chop the apricots in half and set aside. Spoon the meat filling into the pastry case, spreading it out evenly, and then dot the bits of apricot in a pretty concentric pattern on top. Roll any leftover pastry into thin strips and use it as a very loose lattice over the top, brushing the strips with a bit of milk.

Place in the oven for 30 minutes, then reduce the temperature to 160°C/Gas mark 3 and cook for 30 minutes more.

Leave the pie to cool in the tin before slicing it into wedges. It will keep in an airtight container in the fridge for 4–5 days.

Substitute the thyme with...
ROSEMARY, CHIVES, TARRAGON

Eastern-inspired
SLOW ROAST PORK

SERVES: **4-6**
COOKING TIME: **6 HOURS 10 MINUTES**

700g–1kg pork shoulder | 1 tsp cumin seeds | 1 tsp dried coriander leaf
Salt | 1 butternut squash | 2 tsp freshly grated ginger
1 tsp cumin seeds | 2 tbsp chopped coriander, plus extra for serving | Olive oil
125ml rosé wine | 1 heaped tbsp plain flour | 150–200ml chicken stock

Perfect crackling is the holy grail of Sunday lunches, and this method guarantees it every time. The spice combination was inspired by a trip to Istanbul, where I had cumin smoked fish, and the aroma that wafts from the oven after the first couple of hours transports me back there immediately. Still, all you need to know is that the crackling is crackly, the pork is juicy and, not having to peel the squash, this roast dinner could barely be less work.

Preheat the oven to 160°C/Gas mark 3. Score the skin of the pork with a very sharp knife and place in a large roasting tray. In a pestle and mortar, grind together the cumin seeds, dried coriander and a pinch of salt and rub this mixture into the skin, making sure it goes well into the scores. Place the pork in the oven and forget about it for 5 hours – go for a walk or have a nap, don't worry, you've got ages.

Get the squash ready. You don't need to peel it, just top and tail, slice in half lengthways, remove the seeds and cube the flesh. Once the pork has hit the 5-hour mark, scatter the squash in the tray with the ginger, cumin, fresh coriander and a little olive oil if there is not enough juice from the meat to baste it properly. Put everything back in the oven for 1 hour.

Remove the pork from the tray, place it on a plate, cover it with foil and try to resist eating all the crackling before it reaches the table. Put the roasting tray – with the squash still in it – on top of the hob, turning the heat up to high. Pour in the wine and use it to deglaze the pan by scraping the bits off the bottom. Once it has simmered and reduced for 2–3 minutes, add the flour. Stir until it has all been incorporated and then gradually mix in the stock until you have a gravy the consistency you like.

Carve the meat and serve with the squash, gravy and extra coriander leaves, along with any greens that you fancy.

Substitute the coriander with...
PARSLEY, HIBISCUS, LEMON THYME

Clockwise from top left: Various; lavender, parsley, Italian basil; mint; rose

Creamy Mushroom and
CHERVIL STEW

───────────── ● ─────────────

SERVES: **4**
COOKING TIME: **30-35 MINUTES**

───────────── ● ─────────────

2 tbsp olive oil | 250g mushrooms, chopped | 50g frozen peas
1 onion, peeled and finely chopped | 1 red pepper, deseeded and chopped
1 orange pepper, deseeded and chopped | 2 tbsp chopped chervil | Salt
Black pepper | 1 tbsp flour | 200ml vegetable stock | 1 tsp horseradish sauce
1 tbsp Worcestershire sauce (optional) | 100ml double cream

There's nothing very sexy about the word stew, but this one manages to be surprisingly sophisticated. It's the tang of horseradish hidden by the lashings of cream, and the different coloured vegetables that stop this looking like your average brown sludge. Like all stews, this is better the next day, so try to hold back a little sauce to reheat and enjoy as tomorrow's lunch.

Place the oil in a large saucepan with a lid and set over a moderate heat. Add the mushrooms, peas and onion, cover with the lid and let sweat for 5 minutes. Add both peppers, the chervil and some seasoning, give it all a stir and leave to sweat for another 5 minutes.

Add the flour and stir until it has completely dissolved. Pour in the stock and add the horseradish and the Worcestershire sauce if you're using it. Cover with the lid and let everything bubble gently for about 20 minutes until the stock has reduced. Pour in the cream, warming it through without letting it boil, and serve immediately with rice or mashed potato. Any leftovers can be blitzed and made into a brilliant soup for the next day.

Substitute the
chervil with...
BASIL, TARRAGON,
NASTURTIUM

Pan-fried Steak with Mushroom
AND TARRAGON SAUCE

SERVES: **2**
COOKING TIME: **10-15 MINUTES**

50g butter | 50g mushrooms, diced thinly
1 tbsp chopped tarragon | Salt | Black pepper
1 tbsp flour | 250ml milk | 2 x 500g rump steaks

Sometimes you want a supper that will fill you up with only minutes of actual cooking. Steak is just that – I like the meat to make only a fast acquaintance with the pan so that it's all pink and bloody in the middle, but you can of course cook it however you prefer. The sauce is rich and creamy, the piquancy of the tarragon complements the machismo of the meat, and, best of all, it is ready in moments.

Melt the butter in a saucepan and add the mushrooms and tarragon with some seasoning. Let the mushrooms sweat slowly for 4–5 minutes until soft and golden, then add the flour and stir everything together until well combined.

Gradually add the milk, stirring continuously, only allowing the sauce to slowly come to the boil once all the milk has been incorporated.

Meanwhile, heat a heavy-bottomed frying pan until very hot. Fry the steaks in the dry hot pan until done to your liking: allow 1½-2 minutes on each side for rare, 3 minutes on each side for medium, and about 4 minutes on each side for well done. Plate the steaks, pour the sauce over the top and serve with green beans, salad or a portion of chunky chips.

Substitute the tarragon with...
BORAGE, CHIVES, PARSLEY

Substitute the marjoram with...
SAGE, BASIL, THYME

Sausage and
WHITE BEAN BAKE

SERVES: **4-6**
COOKING TIME: **1 HOUR**

25g butter | 1 small leek, chopped | 6 good-quality sausages
1 red pepper, deseeded and chopped | 1 tbsp chopped marjoram
125ml red wine | 200ml beef stock | 1 tbsp tomato purée
400g tin of white beans such as butter or cannellini, drained | Salt | Black pepper

Despite its unglamorous-sounding ingredients, this is perfect for making a big batch of, setting it in the middle of the table and letting guests help themselves to large ladlefuls. Add a bit more stock if you want it to be a chunky soup – it goes beautifully with salty buttered French bread – but it's rich and wonderfully indulgent as it is.

Put the butter into a heavy-bottomed casserole dish with a lid and set it over a medium heat. Once melted, add the leek and let it sweat for 1 minute. Cut the skin of the sausages and squeeze the meat out of the skin and into the dish. Stir the meat as it cooks to help it to break up a bit, and when it begins to brown add the pepper and marjoram.

After about 10 minutes or so the meat should look cooked through and the pepper should be quite soft. Add the wine and turn the heat up, letting the liquid bubble away and reduce. Once it looks like it is drying out, add the stock, tomato purée, the beans, a pinch of salt and a couple of hearty grinds of black pepper. Stir everything together, put the lid on and turn the heat down so that the stew stays at a rolling simmer for 45 minutes.

Serve with a baked sweet potato and your choice of greens – and try to keep a bit in the fridge for the next day. It really will taste even better.

Lamb and Mint
BURGERS

---●---

SERVES: **4**
COOKING TIME: **6-8 MINUTES**

---●---

600g lamb mince | 1 apple, peeled, cored and grated
1 onion, peeled and grated | 2 tbsp chopped mint leaves
Salt | Black pepper | 1 tbsp olive oil

Roast lamb and mint sauce is a classic Sunday combo, so it's no surprise their flavours work well in a humble burger. The addition of the apple makes the patty juicy and sweet and the mint adds pep to this big slab of meat. They can be made several hours in advance and kept in the fridge, and once cooked will be delicious cold the next day too.

Place the lamb, apple, onion, mint and a little seasoning in a large bowl and, with clean hands, squish everything together until well combined. Divide the meat mixture into four equal balls, then squash them between your palms into patty shapes. Place the patties back in the bowl and drizzle them with a little oil, cover with foil and leave them in the fridge for at least 30 minutes to firm up.

Place a large, heavy-bottomed frying pan over a high heat. Once it's really hot, add the burgers and cook for 6–8 minutes. Flip them regularly and press down on them with a flat spatula to help squeeze out the fat as they cook. They are ready once both sides are starting to look well done and crisp. Remove from the pan and serve with a green salad, bread, potato salad and sauces.

Substitute the
mint with...
ROSEMARY, LEMON
THYME, CHIVE

Butternut Squash and Calendula
MAC AND CHEESE

---·---

SERVES: **5-6**
COOKING TIME: **50 MINUTES-1 HOUR**

---·---

1kg butternut squash, peeled, deseeded and cubed | Olive oil
300g dried macaroni | 25g butter | 1½ tbsp plain flour
2 garlic cloves, peeled and chopped | 500ml milk
2 tbsp chopped calendula (marigold) flowers | 1 tbsp Dijon mustard
150g mature cheddar cheese, grated | 50g breadcrumbs

This classic dish has had a resurgence of late and it's not hard to see why. Cheese, pasta, what's not to love? Without wanting to mess with a winning formula too much, I've added just a couple of extra ingredients – the roasted squash lends a subtle nuttiness, whilst the calendula adds a peppery seasoning, with both providing splashes of brightness to an otherwise beige dish. Comfort food at its most colourful.

Preheat the oven to 200°C/Gas mark 6. Place the squash into a roasting dish and drizzle with oil. Roast in the oven for 20–25 minutes until it starts to look golden and caramelised.

Meanwhile, bring a large pan of water to the boil, add a dash of oil and cook the pasta according to the packet instructions. Once cooked, drain the pasta well and set it aside while you make the sauce. Melt the butter in a large saucepan and add the flour and garlic, stirring well to make a paste. Gradually add the milk, a little at a time, stirring continuously until you have a beautiful, smooth sauce.

Add the calendula flowers, mustard and the majority of cheese. Keep an eye on the sauce as it reaches a slow gentle boil, stirring as the cheese melts. Add the pasta to the sauce and combine the two on the heat, giving the pasta a chance to warm up again if it has got a little cold.

Transfer the squash to a 20 x 25cm ovenproof dish and tip all of the pasta and sauce over it. Combine the two as much as you can before sprinkling over the breadcrumbs and the remaining cheese. Bake it in the oven for 30–35 minutes until it's bubbling and the top is brown. Serve immediately.

Substitute the calendula with... OREGANO, THYME, ROSEMARY

Soy-seared Tuna Steaks with
CARROT AND PANSY SALAD

SERVES: **4**
COOKING TIME: **5 MINUTES**

200g carrots, peeled | 200g white cabbage
4 tbsp chopped coriander | 4 tbsp pansy flowers | 2 tbsp olive oil
2 tbsp soy sauce | 4 tuna steaks
For the dressing: Juice of 2 limes | 2 tbsp fish sauce
2 tbsp sesame oil | 4 tbsp soy sauce

You might not normally add pansies – they of country garden fame – to the Eastern-inspired flavours of coriander, sesame and soy, but it's for their impressive colour contrast against the carrot, rather than their taste, which makes them worthy of inclusion. They are slightly sweet, slightly bland, and more like dressing than actual ingredient in their own right. Matched against strong flavours here all they really do is look impressive. Handy, really, as this dish is embarrassingly easy to make.

Slice the carrot and cabbage into really thin strips using a mandolin, potato peeler or knife. Divide the carrot, cabbage, coriander and pansies between four plates, arranging them nicely with the flowers on top.

Put all the dressing ingredients into a jar and shake together to mix well. Set it aside to sit for 1 minute.

Mix together the olive oil and soy sauce and use it to baste each tuna steak liberally. Set a heavy-bottomed frying or griddle pan over a high heat and let it get really hot before adding the fish, searing each side for 1–2 minutes. It will cook quickly but remain a bit pink on the inside. Place a steak on each plate, sliced if you like, drizzle the dressing over the salad and serve.

Substitute the
pansies with...
BASIL, BORAGE,
NASTURTIUM

Desserts

When was the last time you bought a quarter of sweets? You were probably about nine years old, your pocket money just stretching to a bag of rhubarb and custards. The tinkle as the shopkeeper tipped them onto the scales and the eyes-shut hope that you might get more than was strictly a quarter. And you ate them all on the day, because you couldn't get enough of that sugary taste. You probably couldn't manage a whole bag now as adults' tastebuds change – you learn to appreciate depths of flavour and better-quality treats.

That's why herbs and flowers work so well in desserts. Adding rosemary to redcurrants, thyme to strawberry or basil to cherry brings out a taste in the fruit that you never quite realised was there. They add a slightly savoury twist that will turn a conventional pudding into an unusual and intriguing treat.

Gooseberry and Mint
MERINGUE PIE

SERVES: **6**
COOKING TIME: **50 MINUTES**

Flour, for dusting | 500g shortcrust pastry
300g gooseberries, fresh or tinned | 150g sugar | 2 mint sprigs, chopped
100g butter | 4 egg yolks | Finely grated zest and juice of 2 lemons | 25g cornflour
For the meringue: 4 egg whites | 200g caster sugar, plus extra for sprinkling

Tinned fruit has become rather unfashionable, but when you're baking a pie it doesn't really matter how fresh your filling is as it will always look the same once it has been cooked. Fresh gooseberries are so rare now anyway – they're such a pain to pick that growers don't often bother with them – and as mint lasts for so much of the year, you'll want to make this pie more often than just in high summer. I particularly like it in autumn, as the sharp freshness of the berries and mint is like an antidote to the early darkness.

Preheat the oven to 180°C/Gas mark 4. On a lightly floured work surface, roll out the pastry until thin, circular and about 22 x 22cm and transfer it to a 20cm pie dish. Press it into the dish and seal any cracks. Roll the rolling pin over the top to cut away any excess. Cover the pastry with baking paper and weigh it down with baking beans or dried pasta. Place it in the oven and blind bake for 15 minutes. Remove the baking paper and weights and bake for another 10 minutes.

Meanwhile, prepare the filling. If using fresh gooseberries, rinse and top and tail them. If using tinned, drain well. Place in a saucepan with the sugar, mint, butter, egg yolks, lemon zest and juice and place the pan over a low heat. Once the butter has melted and the mixture has begun to bubble, remove a few tablespoons of the liquid and whisk it in a bowl with the cornflour until you have a smooth paste. Return this to the pan and stir it all together – be careful, it may spit. Bring to the boil and pour into the pastry case. Set aside and let cool.

Place the egg whites in the clean, dry bowl of an electric mixer and begin to beat them slowly, adding the caster sugar a little at a time. They should become thick and glossy after about 8 minutes – if stiff peaks form when you lift the beater out of the meringue then it's definitely ready. Carefully spoon it over the gooseberries, using a spatula to spread it out smoothly and evenly. Sprinkle a little extra sugar over the top.

Bake the pie in the oven for 25 minutes until the top of the meringue is pale brown and springy to the touch. Serve immediately, with a generous dollop of cream.

*Substitute the
mint with...*
THYME, ROSEMARY,
ROSE PETALS

Substitute the
mint with...
ROSE PETALS, ROSEMARY,
VIOLET PETALS

Raspberry, Rose and Mint
TIRAMISU

SERVES: **6**
PREPARATION TIME: **20 MINUTES, PLUS CHILLING**

300ml hot Earl Grey tea | 300g sponge fingers | 250g raspberries
4 eggs, separated | 2 tsp rosewater | 2 tbsp chopped mint | 100g sugar
For the sugared rose petals (optional): Rose petals | Milk | Caster sugar

Italians do herbs well. The flash of fresh green basil paired with sun-ripened tomatoes. The earthiness of sage added to a dark sausage casserole. Yet they don't seem to mix them with dessert, which is odd, because the mint in this pudding (inspired by the Italian classic Tiramisu di Fragole) adds a zingy lift. If you're feeling fancy, follow the instructions for sugared rose petals, which are a doddle to make and always look impressive, but don't worry if not, this dish can certainly survive without them.

Place the tea in a bowl and add the sponge fingers to soak for 1–2 minutes, making sure to remove them before they totally disintegrate. Layer half the fingers in a large trifle bowl, or in six individual sundae dishes. Cover with half the raspberries.

In a separate bowl, use an electric hand whisk to beat the egg yolks, rosewater, mint and half the sugar until pale, creamy and at least double in size. This should take about 5 minutes for stiff peaks to have formed, it should stand up when you lift the whisk out of the mixture.

Using an electric mixer and in a clean, dry bowl, beat the egg whites with the remaining sugar until glossy and stiff, this will take about 5 minutes. Gently fold the two egg mixtures together using a metal spoon. Try to combine the two without squashing out too much of the air. Spoon half of this mixture over the raspberries and sponge.

Add another layer of sponge using the remaining fingers, then the rest of the raspberries and finish with the last of the egg mix. Place in the fridge for 1–2 hours to set – this will have a much nicer consistency once chilled.

If you're showing off and want to go down in entertaining history, line a baking tray with greaseproof paper and lay out the washed rose petals. Brush with milk and sprinkle over some sugar. Leave to dry for an hour or so. Delicately throw them over the top of the pudding just before serving.

Strawberry, Rhubarb and
THYME CAKE

●

SERVES: **6-8**
COOKING TIME: **35-55 MINUTES**

●

200g butter, plus extra for greasing | 4 eggs | 200g sugar
1 tbsp chopped thyme | 200g self-raising flour | Milk (optional)
For the filling: 100g rhubarb, chopped
50g strawberries, hulled and halved, plus extra for decorating | 25g sugar
For the buttercream: 250g icing sugar | 80g unsalted butter
1 tbsp milk | 1 tsp vanilla extract

This is a grown up twist on the classic Victoria sponge – the surprising addition of thyme cuts through the sweetness of the fruit. Perfect for a summer balcony party, served with tea or as a lovely partner to a crisp, dry glass of pink fizz. But then, what isn't?

Substitute the thyme with...
LAVENDER, ROSEMARY, LEMON THYME

Preheat the oven to 180°C/Gas mark 4. Grease and line a large 7cm-deep cake tin. Break the eggs into the bowl of an electric mixer, add the sugar and beat until pale and creamy. Add the thyme and butter, sift in the flour and beat until smooth. Add a splash of milk if the mixture is looking a little too solid. Spoon it into the prepared tin and bake in the oven for 35–40 minutes, until golden brown, springy to the touch and it is shrinking away from the edges of the tin. Leave for 5 minutes before removing from the tin and placing on a wire rack to cool.

Once the cake has cooled, make the filling. Add the fruit and sugar to a small pan and place over a high heat, stirring constantly. Nothing will happen for a few seconds and then the sugar should start to melt and the fruit will go a bit gooey. Turn the heat down to low and let it bubble for 10 minutes – it should take on the consistency of thick jam.

Carefully slice the cake in half to create two layers. Spread the filling over the bottom layer, then sandwich the top layer back in place. Make the buttercream by beating all the ingredients together for about 5 minutes, slowly at first and then increasing the speed. It should be thick, pale and creamy. Spread the buttercream all over the top of the cake and decorate with a few strawberries.

Coconut and Coriander
ETON MESS

---•---

SERVES: **4**
COOKING TIME: **10 MINUTES**

---•---

400g pineapple, peeled and chopped | 250ml white wine
100ml double cream | 100ml coconut milk
2 tbsp icing sugar | 2 tbsp chopped coriander | 6 meringue nests

This is one of those puddings where all the parts can be made a bit in advance and then assembled in record time just before serving. If you've got guests coming over then you can whip up the cream ensemble 2–3 hours before you think you'll be serving the pudding – a good thing to do as the noise of the mixer isn't very sociable. I've chosen not to make the meringue from scratch, though of course you can if you want to really show off. The flavours here are tropical, but not overpoweringly so, and it's not quite as sweet as you might imagine. Serve with a good dessert wine.

Place the pineapple in a small saucepan and pour over the wine. Set the pan over a medium heat and let simmer and reduce for about 10 minutes until you're left with the fruit sitting in a sweet, sticky syrup. Set aside to cool.

Using an electric mixer, beat the cream, coconut milk and icing sugar together for about 7 minutes, until it looks like it might be just about to form stiff peaks – for this kind of messy dessert I like the cream to still be a bit soft and floppy. Carefully fold in the coriander using a metal spoon.

Crumble the meringue nests between four separate bowls and spoon the cream on top, finishing each pile off with a large spoonful of pineapple and syrup. Serve immediately.

Substitute the coriander with...
MINT, ROSEMARY, LEMON BALM

Speedy Steamed Sponge with
BASIL AND CHERRY

SERVES: **6**
COOKING TIME: **6-7 MINUTES**

150g butter, plus extra for greasing | 150g self-raising flour
150g soft light brown sugar | 2 eggs | 1 tbsp milk
½ tsp almond essence | 150g cherries (weight pre-stoned)
1½ tbsp chopped basil, plus a few whole leaves for serving | 3 tbsp golden syrup

I'm always comforted by a syrupy steamed sponge pudding, and the fact that this takes just minutes rather than hours to prepare makes it altogether a wonderful, fast fix. The sunshine flavours of the cherry and basil stop this from feeling too much like winter – the perfect pud for summer days that aren't quite as warm as they should be.

In an electric mixer, cream the butter, flour, sugar, eggs, milk and almond essence until it forms a smooth mixture. Stone the cherries and chop into good-sized chunks. Add the cherries pieces and the basil to the batter and gently fold them in using a metal spoon.

Grease a 1-litre pudding bowl and pour the golden syrup into the bottom. Carefully spoon the sponge mixture on top, taking care not to let the syrup and sponge mix too much. Cover the basin – a good-sized plate will do if you don't have a lid – and place the cake in the microwave on full power for 6 minutes. The cake should rise almost to the top, be springy to the touch and a knife inserted into the middle should come out clean. Give the pudding an extra minute if not.

Using a palette knife, carefully ease the knife around the edge of the pudding to loosen, then place a plate on top and turn the pudding upside down, holding the plate with one hand and the bowl with the other. With any luck, the pudding should plop out perfectly. Occasionally I turn it out and it's not quite done at what is now the top – don't worry, just cover it with the bowl and put it back in the microwave for 1 minute. Serve immediately sprinkled with a few basil leaves and double or clotted cream.

Substitute the basil with...
MINT, THYME, ROSEMARY

Honeysuckle and Blackberry
CHEESECAKE

SERVES: **6**
COOKING TIME: **15 MINUTES**

50g honeysuckle flowers, plus extra for decorating | 1 tbsp caster sugar
A small pinch of cinnamon | 150g digestive biscuits
100g butter, melted, plus extra for greasing | 350g cream cheese | 50g icing sugar
300ml double cream | 150g blackberries | Runny honey, for decorating

Nothing beats sucking the nectar out of the honeysuckle flower. A simple countryside pursuit equalled only by picking – and eating – a hedgerow full of blackberries. This pudding combines the two, the big creamy filling only providing a background for their high summer flavours. The taste of the honeysuckle flowers is quite specific, so if you're substituting them for any of my suggestions, just fold the replacement into the cream with the cinnamon rather than making a syrup.

Put the honeysuckle flowers into a saucepan over a high heat with 100ml of water, the caster sugar and the cinnamon. Bring to the boil, turn down the heat and let simmer gently for 15 minutes. Strain the mixture and discard the flowers, you should be left with a couple of tablespoons of syrup – if you are left with lots of water, then bring it back to the boil and reduce it further. Set aside to cool.

Crush the digestive biscuits into crumbs and mix in the butter, combining the two thoroughly. Use a little extra butter to grease a 20cm loose bottomed cake tin and transfer the biscuits into it, pressing them down firmly with the back of a metal spoon so that it becomes one solid biscuit base. Leave it in the fridge for at least 30 minutes to firm up.

Beat together the cream cheese, icing sugar and 1–2 tablespoons of the honeysuckle nectar. In a separate bowl, whisk the cream until it forms big, soft peaks and fold it into the cream cheese mixture using a metal spoon. Pour all of this on top of the biscuit base and decorate the top with the blackberries, adding a drizzle of honey and some extra honeysuckle flowers to decorate. This will keep in the fridge for a couple of days.

Substitute the
honeysuckle with...
MINT, LEMON THYME,
LEMON BALM

Clockwise from top left: Various;
various; thyme, sorrel; hibiscus

*Substitute the
lemon thyme with...*
ROSEMARY, THYME,
MARJORAM

Lemon Thyme and Ginger
CRUMBLE

SERVES: **4-6**
COOKING TIME: **45 MINUTES**

300g plain flour | 175g Demerara sugar
200g butter, softened | 3 pears, cored and chopped
3 nectarines, stones removed and chopped | 2 tbsp crystallised ginger
1 tbsp chopped lemon thyme

Crumble is an enduring favourite, a guaranteed crowd pleaser that is beloved for its winning contrast of crunchy topping and steaming fruit. I like it when the base has a bit of bite too, so I don't cook the fruit first. What makes this special is the way the ginger melts into gooey pockets of sweetness – you can always sprinkle some extra into the crumble mix too.

Preheat the oven to 180°C/Gas mark 4. In a mixing bowl, use your fingers to rub together the flour, sugar and butter until it resembles breadcrumbs. Place the crumble into the fridge to firm up for 10 minutes while you prepare the fruit.

Place the pears and nectarines into a round 20cm ovenproof dish and sprinkle over the ginger and lemon thyme. Roughly mix it all until well combined.

Cover the fruit with the crumble mix and place in the oven for 45 minutes until the fruit starts to bubble up around the sides and the crumble has a nice golden colour on top. Serve immediately with a dollop of double cream or custard.

Redcurrant and Rosemary
DOUBLE CHOCOLATE BROWNIES

———— • ————

MAKES: **12 SQUARES**
COOKING TIME: **35-45 MINUTES**

———— • ————

300g butter, plus extra for greasing | 400g dark chocolate
5 eggs | 400g sugar | 100g self-raising flour
25g cocoa | 50g redcurrants, stalks removed
100g white chocolate, broken into chunks | 1 sprig rosemary, leaves only

The mark of a good brownie is that it should be ridiculously gooey in the middle – there is nothing sadder than one that has more in common with cake than it does unbaked batter. This recipe will ensure that the brownies are messy and sticky in the centre, just as they should be. I like the redcurrants and rosemary, which give them the pretence of being a bit more grown up than just chocolaty goodness, but you can leave them out if you simply want a sugary fix.

Preheat the oven to 180°C/Gas mark 4 and grease a 30 x 20cm baking dish. Break the dark chocolate into a heatproof glass bowl and add the butter. Melt the two together by setting the bowl over a pan of boiling water, making sure that the water does not touch the bottom of the bowl. Or you can melt them in the microwave; just keep an eye on it to prevent it from burning.

Meanwhile, beat the eggs and sugar together until light and fluffy. Sift in the flour and cocoa and fold it all together using a metal spoon until well combined. Gently fold in the melted chocolate mixture, followed by the redcurrants, chunks of white chocolate and rosemary leaves.

Spoon the mixture into the prepared dish and bake in the oven for 30–35 minutes. You want the top to look a little like a crust, but the middle to still be gooey and only slightly resemble a cakey consistency. Leave the brownies to cool in the tray for a few minutes before cutting them into squares, then lift them out and set on a wire rack to continue to cool. Just try not to eat them all at once.

Substitute the
rosemary with...
MINT, THYME, BASIL

*Substitute the
winter savory
with...*

ROSEMARY, HIBISCUS,
LEMON THYME

Winter Fruit Salad with
WINTER SAVORY

SERVES: **4**
COOKING TIME: **10 MINUTES**

25g butter | 2 tbsp runny honey
2 sprigs of winter savory, leaves only | A pinch of cinnamon
4 pears, cored and sliced | 4 Braeburn apples, cored and cubed
50g black seedless grapes, halved | 50g red grapes, halved
Seeds of 1 pomegranate | 3 tbsp Grand Marnier

Winter savory is one of the lesser known herbs, but at a time of year when fresh produce is mainly cabbage and root vegetables it makes sense to add as many flavours as you possibly can. It has a beautifully pungent aroma but the flavour diminishes when cooked, which is why the light simmer here is the best method to help retain some of its taste.

Put the butter, honey, winter savory and cinnamon in a large saucepan over a medium heat. Once everything has melted together, add the pears, apples, grapes and pomegranate seeds and make sure all the fruit is well coated in the syrup.

Add the Grand Marnier and let everything simmer for 5–7 minutes more – you want the fruit to still have a bit of crunch. Serve warm or allow to cool, but either way this goes well with a good-quality vanilla ice cream.

Hibiscus and Orange
CUSTARD TART

SERVES: **6-8**
COOKING TIME: **1 HOUR 5 MINUTES**

Flour, for dusting | 500g shortcrust pastry
For the filling: 300ml milk | 200ml double cream
Finely grated zest of 1 orange | 2 tsp orange blossom water or juice of ½ an orange
2 eggs plus 2 extra egg yolks | 100g sugar | 6 hibiscus flowers

Hibiscus flowers are surprisingly tangy and have a sharpness that works just as well with meat as in desserts. Mexicans use them in enchiladas, but I like them to spice up the traditional English custard tart, the softness of the pie filling taking well to their zesty zing. Plus they look pretty, too, which is always a bonus when you're showing off for guests.

Preheat the oven to 200°C/Gas mark 6. On a lightly floured work surface, roll out the pastry until thin and about 22 x 22cm. Shuffle your hands under the pastry, palms facing up and fingers spread wide and transfer it to a 20cm round tin. Press it into the edges and roll the rolling pin over the top to cut off any excess. Cover the pastry with a circle of baking paper and weigh it down with baking beans, dried pasta or rice and blind bake for 15 minutes. Remove the paper and weights and returning the pastry to the oven for another 5 minutes. Set aside to cool.

Place all of the filling ingredients except for the hibiscus flours in a large saucepan and set the pan over a medium heat, stirring constantly as the sugar dissolves. Gradually bring the mixture to the boil and let thicken slightly – after 3–4 minutes of simmering it should coat the back of a spoon. Pour into the pastry case. Float the flowers on top of the custard and bake the tart in the oven for 40 minutes, until the custard is golden and set. Serve it hot or cold, with cream or ice cream.

Substitute the hibiscus with...
LAVENDER, ROSE, ROSEMARY

Peanut Butter and
OREGANO COOKIES

MAKES: **12-14**
COOKING TIME: **12-15 MINUTES**

175g butter, melted, plus extra for greasing | 250g plain flour
½ tsp bicarbonate of soda | 300g light brown sugar
1 tbsp golden syrup | 1 egg | 2 tbsp crunchy peanut butter
1 tbsp chopped oregano | 1 tbsp milk (if needed) | Unsalted peanuts, for decorating

I've never heard of using peanuts with oregano before, but something told me the soft fragrance of the herb would work subtly with the saltiness of peanut butter and sweetness of the syrup. These cookies are surprisingly nice – they are gooey, chewy and delicately unusual and go brilliantly with a cup of tea at 4pm.

Preheat the oven to 180°C/Gas mark 4. Grease 1 large or 2 medium baking trays. Mix together all the ingredients apart from the milk and unsalted peanuts in a food processor. If the mixture looks a little too dry and firm, add the milk and mix again. Using clean hands, shape the dough into about 12–14 small patties and spread them over the baking tray or trays, pressing 2–3 peanuts into the top of each one.

Place in the oven for 12–15 minutes, until the cookies are golden and have slightly spread. Try not to overcook them as you want them to be quite gooey in the middle. Transfer to a wire rack to cool. These can be kept in an airtight container for 3–4 days if you can resist eating them all at once.

Substitute the oregano with...
MINT, BASIL,
LEMON THYME

Violet Scones with
HONEYED CREAM

●

MAKES: **12 SCONES**
COOKING TIME: **12-15 MINUTES**

●

50g butter, plus extra for greasing | 225g self-raising flour, plus extra for dusting
25g sugar | 150ml milk, plus extra for glazing
1 tsp vanilla extract | 3 violet flowers, chopped, plus extra petals for serving
100g clotted cream | 2 tbsp runny honey

I've never been a fan of the soapy taste of parma violets, but if you use violet flowers sparingly and bake them they are far subtler – a clever floral note rather than an overpowering flavour. The honeyed cream is what provides the real sweetness here; it's thick and indulgent and removes the need for jam or butter… although a dollop of lemon curd goes well if you have a really sweet tooth.

Preheat the oven to 225°C/Gas mark 7 and line and grease a large baking tray. In a food processor, mix together the flour, butter and sugar until it resembles breadcrumbs. Pour in the milk and vanilla extract and beat into a stiff dough. Add the violet flowers and give a final few pulses of the processor to combine them into the mixture.

Lightly dust your worktop with flour and place the dough in the middle, sprinkling a little flour over the top. Using a rolling pin, work the dough until it's about 2cm thick. Take a 5cm round cutter and cut out discs, placing them onto the baking tray. Roll the leftover dough out again and cut out more rounds, repeating until all the dough is used up. Try not to roll the dough too many times as this will lead to tough scones. Brush the top of each with a dab of milk and place the tray in the oven for 12–15 minutes until golden. Transfer to a wire rack and leave to cool.

Just before you are about to eat the scones, place the cream in a small bowl and briefly fold in the honey – do not mix until combined, you want it to have a rippled effect – and top with a few violet petals. Cut open the scones, spread a bit of cream on top and serve.

Substitute the violet with...

LAVENDER, ROSEMARY, ROSE PETALS

Honey and Basil
BAKED PEAR

---•---

SERVES: **4**
COOKING TIME: **20 MINUTES**

---•---

4 pears | 2 tbsp golden or normal sultanas
2 tbsp light brown sugar | 3 large basil leaves, torn
4 tsp runny honey | demerara sugar, for sprinkling

Baked apples are a staunch 1970s' concoction, but just because the concept is dated, doesn't necessarily make it wrong. Using pears and basil feels a bit more contemporary, but it doesn't stop the dessert from feeling comfortingly familiar. You can, of course, use any dried fruit – I chose golden sultanas only because they look the prettiest. Dried cranberries are a good bet, too.

Preheat the oven to 180°C/Gas mark 4. Wash and core the pears using an apple corer so that the core is removed but the pear is left whole. Using a sharp knife, score a shallow line around the widest part of the pears. Stand the pears upright in a roasting dish.

In a bowl, mix together the sultanas, brown sugar and basil, before spooning the mixture evenly down the holes in the middle of each pear. Drizzle a teaspoon of honey over the top of each and let it run down the sides. Sprinkle a bit of demerara sugar over the top and bake the fruit in the oven for 20 minutes until soft and golden. Leave the pears to cool momentarily before serving them covered in double cream or with a big spoonful of vanilla ice cream.

Substitute the basil with...

THYME, OREGANO,
ROSEMARY

Clockwise from top left: Lavender;
African violets; rosemary; sage, mint,
basil; sorrel

Autumn
PUDDING

SERVES: **6**
COOKING TIME: **10 MINUTES**

2 sweet apples, such as Braeburn, cored | 400g plums, stoned
2 juicy pears, such as William, cored | 400g blackberries
2 sprigs of thyme, plus extra for serving | 200g sugar
8–10 slices of white bread, crusts cut off

I love the sweet, summery flavours of the classic British summer pudding, all kept moist and gooey by soaking the bread – it's always seems impressive when anyone actually bothers to make one. It was the recipe writer Lucas Hollweg who first suggested to me that the pudding could transcend the seasons, swapping high summer berries for soft early autumn fruit. I've gone a step further and thrown in the pear and some thyme which really makes this a serious dessert, the herb counteracting the sweetness of the fruit. The whole thing evokes the full September hedgerow, and will stop you from lamenting the departure of summer.

Chop the apple, plums and pear into chunks that are roughly the size of the blackberries. Place all of the fruit in a large saucepan with the thyme and sugar. Add 75ml of water and set over a low heat. Cook for about 10 minutes until the fruit is soft and the sugar has dissolved. Strain the mixture with a jug set below to catch all the juice. Set the fruit aside to cool.

Lay a slice of bread on your work surface and press the bottom of a 1-litre pudding bowl on top of it. The circular imprint of the base should be on the bread; cut it out. Press the bread circle into the bottom of the bowl. Set one slice of bread aside for later and use the remaining slices to line the sides, pressing them together so that they overlap and are sealed. Once you have lined the entire bowl, cut off any bread that overlaps the top and set the trimmings aside for later. Pour most of the fruit juice carefully over the bread so that it turns red and you can't see any white.

Spoon the fruit into the bread bowl until it reaches the top. Place the last slice of bread on top, using any leftover slithers to fill any gaps, and pour over the remaining juice. Place a small weighted bowl on top of the pudding and leave the whole thing to set in the fridge for 2–3 hours or overnight.

To serve, place a plate over the top and carefully turn the pudding upside down to tip it out onto the plate. Slice into portions and place in bowls. Add some double cream and garnish with a sprig of thyme.

Substitute the
thyme with...
BASIL, MINT,
ROSEMARY

Drinks

Other than providing ingredients for your recipes, the best thing about a herb garden is being able to sit out in it – admiring the colours and fragrance, spotting bees drone lazily past or having a drink in the early evening sunlight.

Herbs and flowers lend themselves to drinks. Used for centuries as teas, they're so much more versatile than we imagine. The brilliance of mint in a mojito is well documented, but there are plenty of other cocktails that work just as beautifully.

A few of these recipes require a bit of overnight infusion, but some are so simple you can keep making them all night, refreshing glasses no matter how unsteady you get. There are non-alcoholic coolers too, but few would judge you if you added a slug of the spirit of your choice.

As with every recipe, botanical notes are there to enhance the flavour, but with drinks you can pretty much add any herb or flower you have to hand. Experiment, change the flavours, enjoy yourself. That's what drinking is all about, after all.

Substitute the mint with...
ROSEMARY, BASIL,
SUMMER SAVORY

Minty
SPRITZ

---•---

SERVES: **1**

---•---

2–3 mint leaves | A splash of Aperol, about 2 tsp | Prosecco

The Italian digestif Aperol is enjoying a bit of a renassiance at the moment – popping up in current cocktail favourite Negroni or with Prosecco and soda to make a Spritz. Its orangey, bitter taste is less harsh than Campari but takes the sweet edge off the fizz. I've ditched the soda, which isn't really needed, and added the mint, which tastes so fresh and summery it's like drinking Pimm's. Dangerous.

Place the mint leaves in the bottom of a champagne flute or coupe and add a splash of Aperol. Top the glass up with Prosecco and drink immediately.

When you're doing refills you can add fresh mint if you like, but the original leaves will still hold enough taste to flavour subsequent drinks – and make the whole process even easier.

Geranium SUNSET

●

MAKES: **ABOUT 1 LITRE**

●

225g watermelon, skin removed and flesh chopped into cubes
3 scented geranium (pelargonium) leaves | 600ml smooth orange juice
Vodka or tequila (optional)

Pelargoniums, or geraniums as they are commonly called, were the first plants on my balcony. Whilst watering them in the evening, I enjoyed some of the most beautiful sunsets I've ever seen. I created this drink in homage to the vibrant pinks, oranges, reds and yellows of my flowers that were reflected overhead in the most painterly of ways. And a happy coincidence is that adding a shot of booze makes them perfect to have at sundown, too. Make sure you use scented pelargonium leaves, which are edible, for this recipe.

Remove any black seeds from the watermelon and blitz it in a blender until smooth. Strain the watermelon pulp into a jug through a fine sieve and add the scented geranium leaves to the jug. Mix and muddle them a bit with a stick or wooden spoon, cover with cling film and leave for a couple of hours or overnight in the fridge.

When you're ready to serve, remove the geranium leaves and put a couple of tablespoons of watermelon juice in the bottom of a hi-ball glass, topping up with the orange juice. If you slowly pour the orange in over the back of a spoon, the drink should become streaked with pink and yellow. Serve immediately – with a shot of vodka or tequila added if you fancy it.

Substitute the geranium with...
VIOLET, MINT,
ROSE PETALS

Elderflower and
LEMON THYME-ADE

MAKES: **ABOUT 1 LITRE**

125ml elderflower cordial **|** 3 sprigs of lemon thyme
Ice cubes, for serving

You might think it's cheating to use elderflower cordial – I call it a time-saving tip. I find that the lemon thyme gives this drink an unusual and homemade flavour, balancing the sweetness to make it more interesting. Honestly, the lemon thyme really adds a flourish, so don't feel guilty about using cordial.

Put the cordial into a small saucepan with the lemon thyme. Bring it to the boil and let simmer for 2 minutes.

Lift the pan from the heat and using a slotted spoon, remove the lemon thyme from the liquid and discard. Pour the cordial into a large jug or punch bowl. Add 1 litre of cold water, some ice cubes and serve in glasses.

Substitute the lemon thyme with...
MINT, LAVENDER, OREGANO

Raspberry Basil
COOLER

SERVES: 1

100g raspberries, plus extra for serving | 1 tbsp sugar | Juice of ½ lime
3 basil leaves, plus extra for serving | Ice cubes, for serving

A big pitcher of this makes for a very pleasant way to cool down on a hot afternoon. Keep the cordial base undiluted in the fridge for up to a week – just put it in an airtight bottle. Add a bit of ginger ale and vodka to make an equally delicious Raspberry Mule.

In a small pan, simmer the raspberries, sugar, lime juice and basil until the sugar has dissolved, the raspberries are nothing but a big mush and you can smell the aromatic basil. Pass the mixture through a fine sieve into a measuring jug, pressing it through with a metal spoon. Leave to cool.

Pour 3 parts cold water to 1 part raspberry cordial (about 150ml of water and 50ml of cordial) into a long glass. To serve, add some ice cubes, a few raspberries and a basil leaf for good measure.

Substitute the basil with...
MINT, ROSEMARY,
LEMON THYME

Substitute the dill with...

BASIL, MINT,
CHERVIL

Dill and Cucumber
GIN

MAKES: **ABOUT 1 LITRE**

1 litre gin | Half a cucumber, chopped into short batons
4–5 dill fronds | Tonic or cloudy lemonade, for serving

There are not enough ways to describe how wonderful this gin infusion is. The dill brings out all the botanicals in the booze whilst the cucumber keeps it refreshing, light and summery. You can scale it down if you don't want to make a whole litre – as long as there are a couple of bits of dill and at least two or three slices of cucumber you'll be able to taste the difference – but trust me one, two, or even three of these is never enough.

Pour the gin into a container large enough for you to be able to add the other ingredients. Throw in the cucumber and dill, cover and leave in the fridge overnight.

Use the infusion as the base for a gin and tonic, or with cloudy lemonade for a long, cool drink. The infused gin will keep in the fridge for up to 1 week – feel free to leave the cucumber and dill floating happily in it.

Rhubarb and Savory
STORM

SERVES: **1**
COOKING TIME: **10 MINUTES**

250g rhubarb, trimmed and chopped | 50g sugar
1 large sprig of summer savory
Ice cubes, for serving | 25ml dark rum
Ginger beer, for serving

This fruity take on the classic Dark and Stormy cocktail (rum and ginger) takes the harshness off the rum and instead adds a subtle hint of layered sweetness, with the aromatic savory just detectable underneath. A great pre-dinner appetiser, the ginger works as a palette cleanser, and the rum…well, the rum does its job nicely.

Place the rhubarb in a saucepan with the sugar, savory and at least 50ml of water and set over a high heat. Once boiling and the sugar has melted, turn it down to a simmer and let it bubble away for about 10 minutes, until the rhubarb is soft.

Pass the rhubarb through a metal sieve set over a jug, pressing it against the mesh with a metal spoon to get out all of the liquid. You should have about 150ml of syrup from this, if not then put the rhubarb mush back in the pan, add some more water and bring it back to the boil. Pass it through the sieve again to make up the 150ml of syrup. You can set aside the stewed rhubarb to eat later – it goes nicely with a splash of cream. Place the jug of rhubarb syrup in the fridge to cool.

When ready to serve, put some ice in a short glass, add the rum and 25ml of the rhubarb syrup. Add some ginger beer, topping it up as much as you'd like, and drink immediately.

Substitute the
summer savory
with...
ROSEMARY, THYME,
WINTER SAVORY

Index

Acknowledgements

A big thank you to everyone at Quadrille, whose hard work and support made this project not just possible but so much fun. Alison Cathie, Jane O'Shea, Louise McKeever, Helen Lewis, Claire Peters, Emily Lapworth, Alex Elliott, Hillary Farley, and of course, Ed Griffiths and Yvonne Doolan.

Huge appreciation for Yuki Suguira, Alice Hart, Kim Lightbody and Bear, whose dedication and vision on the shoots and support throughout the whole book turned this into the most rewarding and enjoyable thing I've done in my career. Tom Winchester, Fiona Ellis, the Dudgeons and the

Tylers for lending their gardens, kitchens and time, and Sarah Bailey and Saska Graville at Red for their unwavering encouragement.

Whilst I'm feeling the love, thanks to Tiffanie Darke, Kara O'Reilly, Neil McLennan and Lorna V for teaching me everything I know about publishing, without which I'd never have got this written.

And Will Tyler, for letting me turn our balcony into a herb garden, being a willing taster, and for generally being amazing.